Apache Hive Essentials
Second Edition

Essential techniques to help you process, and get unique insights from, big data

Dayong Du

BIRMINGHAM - MUMBAI

Apache Hive Essentials
Second Edition

Copyright © 2018 Packt Publishing

Commissioning Editor: Amey Varangaonkar
Acquisition Editor: Noyonika Das
Content Development Editor: Mohammed Yusuf Imaratwale
Technical Editor: Jinesh Topiwala
Copy Editor: Safis Editing
Project Coordinator: Hardik Bhinde
Proofreader: Safis Editing
Indexer: Rekha Nair
Graphics: Jason Monteiro
Production Coordinator: Aparna Bhagat

First published: February 2015
Second edition: June 2018

Production reference: 1290618

Published by Packt Publishing Ltd.
Livery Place
35 Livery Street
Birmingham
B3 2PB, UK.

ISBN 978-1-78899-509-2

www.packtpub.com

I dedicate this book to my daughter, Elaine

`mapt.io`

Mapt is an online digital library that gives you full access to over 5,000 books and videos, as well as industry leading tools to help you plan your personal development and advance your career. For more information, please visit our website.

Why subscribe?

- Spend less time learning and more time coding with practical eBooks and Videos from over 4,000 industry professionals

- Improve your learning with Skill Plans built especially for you

- Get a free eBook or video every month

- Mapt is fully searchable

- Copy and paste, print, and bookmark content

PacktPub.com

Did you know that Packt offers eBook versions of every book published, with PDF and ePub files available? You can upgrade to the eBook version at `www.PacktPub.com` and, as a print book customer, you are entitled to a discount on the eBook copy. Get in touch with us at `service@packtpub.com` for more details.

At `www.PacktPub.com`, you can also read a collection of free technical articles, sign up for a range of free newsletters, and receive exclusive discounts and offers on Packt books and eBooks.

Contributors

About the author

Dayong Du is a big data practitioner, author, and coach with over 10 years' experience in technology consulting, designing, and implementing enterprise big data architecture and analytics in various industries, including finance, media, travel, and telecoms. He has a master's degree in computer science from Dalhousie University and is a Cloudera certified Hadoop developer. He is a cofounder of Toronto Big Data Professional Association and the founder of DataFiber.com.

About the reviewers

Deepak Kumar Sahu is a big data technology-driven professional with extensive experience in data gathering, modeling, analysis, validation, and architecture design to build next-generation analytics platforms. He has a strong analytical and technical background with good problem-solving skills to develop effective, complex business solutions. He enjoys developing high-quality software and designing secure and scalable data systems. He has written blogs on machine learning, data science, big data management, and Blockchain. He can be reached at linkedin `deepakkumarsahu`.

Shuguang Li is a big data professional with extensive experience in designing and implementing complete end-to-end Hadoop infrastructure using MapReduce, Spark, Hive, Atlas, Kafka, Sqoop, HBase. The whole lifecycle covers data ingestion, data streaming, data analyzing and data mining. He also has hands on experience in blockchain technology, including fabric and sawtooth. Shuguang has more than 20 years' experience in financial industry, like banks, stock exchange and mutual fund companies. He can be reach at linkedin `michael-li-12016915`.

Packt is searching for authors like you

If you're interested in becoming an author for Packt, please visit `authors.packtpub.com` and apply today. We have worked with thousands of developers and tech professionals, just like you, to help them share their insight with the global tech community. You can make a general application, apply for a specific hot topic that we are recruiting an author for, or submit your own idea.

Table of Contents

Preface

With an increasing interest in big data analysis, Hive over Hadoop becomes a cutting-edge data solution for storing, computing, and analyzing big data. The SQL-like syntax makes Hive easier to learn and is popularly accepted as a standard for interactive SQL queries over big data. The variety of features available within Hive provides us with the capability of doing complex big data analysis without advanced coding skills. The maturity of Hive lets it gradually merge and share its valuable architecture and functionalities across different computing frameworks beyond Hadoop.

Apache Hive Essentials, Second Edition prepares your journey to big data by covering the introduction of backgrounds and concepts in the big data domain, along with the process of setting up and getting familiar with your Hive working environment in the first two chapters. In the next four chapters, the book guides you through discovering and transforming the value behind big data using examples and skills of Hive query languages. In the last four chapters, the book highlights the well-selected and advanced topics, such as performance, security, and extensions, as exciting adventures for this worthwhile big data journey.

Who this book is for

If you are a data analyst, developer, or user who wants to use Hive for exploring and analyzing data in Hadoop, this is the right book for you. Whether you are new to big data or already an experienced user, you will be able to master both basic and advanced functions of Hive. Since HQL is quite similar to SQL, some previous experience with SQL and databases will help with getting a better understanding of this book.

What this book covers

Chapter 1, *Overview of Big Data and Hive*, begins with the evolution of big data, Hadoop ecosystem, and Hive. You will also learn the Hive architecture and advantages of using Hive in big data analysis.

Chapter 2, *Setting Up the Hive Environment*, presents the Hive environment setup and configuration. It also covers using Hive through the command line and development tools.

Chapter 3, *Data Definition and Description*, outlines the basic data types and data definition language for tables, partitions, buckets, and views in Hive.

Chapter 4, *Data Correlation and Scope*, shows you ways to discover the data by querying, linking, and scoping the data in Hive.

Chapter 5, *Data Manipulation*, focuses on the process of exchanging, moving, sorting, and transforming the data in Hive.

Chapter 6, *Data Aggregation and Sampling*, explains the way of doing aggregation and sample using aggregation functions, analytic functions, windowing, and sample clauses.

Chapter 7, *Performance Considerations*, introduces the best practices of performance considerations in the aspect of design, file format, compression, storage, query, and job.

Chapter 8, *Extensibility Considerations*, describes the way of extending Hive by creating user-defined functions, streaming, serializers, and deserializers.

Chapter 9, *Security Considerations*, introduces the area of Hive security in terms of authentication, authorization, and encryption.

Chapter 10, *Working with Other Tools*, discusses how Hive works with other big data tools.

To get the most out of this book

This book will give you maximum benefit if you have some experience with SQL. If you are a data analyst, developer, or simply someone who wants to quickly get started with Hive to explore and analyze Big Data in Hadoop, this is the book for you. Additionally, install the following in your system.

- JDK 1.8
- Hadoop 2.x.y
- Ubuntu 16.04/CentOS 7

Download the example code files

You can download the example code files for this book from your account at www.packtpub.com. If you purchased this book elsewhere, you can visit www.packtpub.com/support and register to have the files emailed directly to you.

You can download the code files by following these steps:

1. Log in or register at www.packtpub.com.
2. Select the **SUPPORT** tab.
3. Click on **Code Downloads & Errata**.
4. Enter the name of the book in the **Search** box and follow the onscreen instructions.

Once the file is downloaded, please make sure that you unzip or extract the folder using the latest version of:

- WinRAR/7-Zip for Windows
- Zipeg/iZip/UnRarX for Mac
- 7-Zip/PeaZip for Linux

The code bundle for the book is also hosted on GitHub at https://github.com/ PacktPublishing/Apache-Hive-Essentials-Second-Edition. In case there's an update to the code, it will be updated on the existing GitHub repository.

We also have other code bundles from our rich catalog of books and videos available at https://github.com/PacktPublishing/. Check them out!

Download the color images

We also provide a PDF file that has color images of the screenshots/diagrams used in this book. You can download it here: http://www.packtpub.com/sites/default/files/downloads/ApacheHiveEssentialsSecon dEdition_ColorImages.pdf.

Conventions used

There are a number of text conventions used throughout this book.

CodeInText: Indicates code words in text, database table names, folder names, filenames, file extensions, pathnames, dummy URLs, user input, and Twitter handles. Here is an example: "Add the necessary system path variables in the ~/.profile or ~/.bashrc file"

A block of code is set as follows:

```
export HADOOP_HOME=/opt/hadoop
export HADOOP_CONF_DIR=/opt/hadoop/conf
export HIVE_HOME=/opt/hive
export HIVE_CONF_DIR=/opt/hive/conf
export PATH=$PATH:$HIVE_HOME/bin:$HADOOP_HOME/
bin:$HADOOP_HOME/sbin
```

Any command-line or beeline interactive input or output is written as follows:

```
$hive
$beeline -u "jdbc:hive2://localhost:10000"
```

Bold: Indicates a new term, an important word, or words that you see onscreen. For example, words in menus or dialog boxes appear in the text like this. Here is an example: "Select **Preference** from the interface."

Warnings or important notes appear like this.

Tips and tricks appear like this.

Get in touch

Feedback from our readers is always welcome.

General feedback: Email feedback@packtpub.com and mention the book title in the subject of your message. If you have questions about any aspect of this book, please email us at questions@packtpub.com.

Errata: Although we have taken every care to ensure the accuracy of our content, mistakes do happen. If you have found a mistake in this book, we would be grateful if you would report this to us. Please visit www.packtpub.com/submit-errata, selecting your book, clicking on the Errata Submission Form link, and entering the details.

Piracy: If you come across any illegal copies of our works in any form on the internet, we would be grateful if you would provide us with the location address or website name. Please contact us at copyright@packtpub.com with a link to the material.

If you are interested in becoming an author: If there is a topic that you have expertise in and you are interested in either writing or contributing to a book, please visit authors.packtpub.com.

Reviews

Please leave a review. Once you have read and used this book, why not leave a review on the site that you purchased it from? Potential readers can then see and use your unbiased opinion to make purchase decisions, we at Packt can understand what you think about our products, and our authors can see your feedback on their book. Thank you!

For more information about Packt, please visit packtpub.com.

1
Overview of Big Data and Hive

This chapter is an overview of big data and Hive, especially in the Hadoop ecosystem. It briefly introduces the evolution of big data so that readers know where they are in the journey of big data and can find out their preferred areas in future learning. This chapter also covers how Hive has become one of the leading tools in the big data ecosystem and why it is still competitive.

In this chapter, we will cover the following topics:

- A short history from the database, data warehouse to big data
- Introducing big data
- Relational and NoSQL databases versus Hadoop
- Batch, real-time, and stream processing
- Hadoop ecosystem overview
- Hive overview

A short history

In the 1960s, when computers became a more cost-effective option for businesses, people started to use databases to manage data. Later on, in the 1970s, relational databases became more popular for business needs since they connected physical data with the logical business easily and closely. In the next decade, **Structured Query Language** (**SQL**) became the standard query language for databases. The effectiveness and simplicity of SQL motivated lots of people to use databases and brought databases closer to a wide range of users and developers. Soon, it was observed that people used databases for data application and management and this continued for a long period of time.

Once plenty of data was collected, people started to think about how to deal with the historical data. Then, the term data warehousing came up in the 1990s. From that time onward, people started discussing how to evaluate current performance by reviewing the historical data. Various data models and tools were created to help enterprises effectively manage, transform, and analyze their historical data. Traditional relational databases also evolved to provide more advanced aggregation and analyzed functions as well as optimizations for data warehousing. The leading query language was still SQL, but it was more intuitive and powerful compared to the previous versions. The data was still well-structured and the model was normalized. As we entered the 2000s, the internet gradually became the topmost industry for the creation of the majority of data in terms of variety and volume. Newer technologies, such as social media analytics, web mining, and data visualizations, helped lots of businesses and companies process massive amounts of data for a better understanding of their customers, products, competition, and markets. The data volume grew and the data format changed faster than ever before, which forced people to search for new solutions, especially in the research and open source areas. As a result, big data became a hot topic and a challenging field for many researchers and companies.

However, in every challenge there lies great opportunity. In the 2010s, Hadoop, which was one of the big data open source projects, started to gain wide attention due to its open source license, active communities, and power to deal with the large volumes of data. This was one of the few times that an open source project led to the changes in technology trends before any commercial software products. Soon after, the NoSQL database, real-time analytics, and machine learning, as followers, quickly became important components on top of the Hadoop big data ecosystem. Armed with these big data technologies, companies were able to review the past, evaluate the current, and grasp the future opportunities.

Introducing big data

Big Data is not simply a big volume of data. Here, the word **Big** refers to the big scope of data. A well-known saying in this domain is to describe big data with the help of three words starting with the letter V: volume, velocity, and variety. But the analytical and data science world has seen data varying in other dimensions in addition to the fundament three Vs of big data, such as veracity, variability, volatility, visualization, and value. The different Vs mentioned so far are explained as follows:

- **Volume**: This refers to the amount of data generated in seconds. 90% of the world's data today has been created in the last two years. Since that time, the data in the world doubles every two years. Such big volumes of data are mainly generated by machines, networks, social media, and sensors, including structured, semi-structured, and unstructured data.

- **Velocity**: This refers to the speed at which the data is generated, stored, analyzed, and moved around. With the availability of internet-connected devices, wireless or wired machines and sensors can pass on their data as soon as it is created. This leads to real-time data streaming and helps businesses to make valuable and fast decisions.

- **Variety**: This refers to the different data formats. Data used to be stored in the `.txt`, `.csv`, and `.dat` formats from data sources such as filesystems, spreadsheets, and databases. This type of data, which resides in a fixed field within a record or file, is called structured data. Nowadays, data is not always in the traditional structured format. The newer semi-structured or unstructured forms of data are also generated by various methods such as email, photos, audio, video, PDFs, SMSes, or even something we have no idea about. These varieties of data formats create problems for storing and analyzing data. This is one of the major challenges we need to overcome in the big data domain.

- **Veracity**: This refers to the quality of data, such as trustworthiness, biases, noise, and abnormality in data. Corrupted data is quite normal. It could originate due to a number of reasons, such as typos, missing or uncommon abbreviations, data reprocessing, and system failures. However, ignoring this malicious data could lead to inaccurate data analysis and eventually a wrong decision. Therefore, making sure the data is correct in terms of data audition and correction is very important for big data analysis.

- **Variability**: This refers to the changing of data. It means that the same data could have different meanings in different contexts. This is particularly important when carrying out sentiment analysis. The analysis algorithms are able to understand the context and discover the exact meaning and values of data in that context.

- **Volatility**: This refers to how long the data is valid and stored. This is particularly important for real-time analysis. It requires a target time window of data to be determined so that analysts can focus on particular questions and gain good performance out of the analysis.

- **Visualization**: This refers to the way of making data well understood. Visualization does not only mean ordinary graphs or pie charts; it also makes vast amounts of data comprehensible in a multidimensional view that is easy to understand. Visualization is an innovative way to show changes in data. It requires lots of interaction, conversations, and joint efforts between big data analysts and business-domain experts to make the visualization meaningful.

- **Value**: This refers to the knowledge gained from data analysis on big data. The value of big data is how organizations turn themselves into big data-driven companies and use the insight from big data analysis for their decision-making.

In summary, big data is not just about lots of data, it is a practice to discover new insight from existing data and guide the analysis of new data. A big-data-driven business will be more agile and competitive to overcome challenges and win competitions.

The relational and NoSQL databases versus Hadoop

To better understand the differences among the relational database, NoSQL database, and Hadoop, let's compare them with ways of traveling. You will be surprised to find that they have many similarities. When people travel, they either take cars or airplanes, depending on the travel distance and cost. For example, when you travel to Vancouver from Toronto, an airplane is always the first choice in terms of the travel time versus cost. When you travel to Niagara Falls from Toronto, a car is always a good choice. When you travel to Montreal from Toronto, some people may prefer taking a car to an airplane. The distance and cost here are like the big data volume and investment. The traditional relational database is like the car, and the Hadoop big data tool is like the airplane. When you deal with a small amount of data (short distance), a relational database (like the car) is always the best choice, since it is fast and agile to deal with a small or moderate amount of data. When you deal with a big amount of data (long distance), Hadoop (like the airplane) is the best choice, since it is more linear-scalable, fast, and stable to deal with the big volume of data. You could drive from Toronto to Vancouver, but it takes too much time. You can also take an airplane from Toronto to Niagara Falls, but it would take more time on your way to the airport and cost more than traveling by car. In addition, you could take a ship or a train. This is like a NoSQL database, which offers characteristics and balance from both a relational database and Hadoop in terms of good performance and various data format support for moderate to large amounts of data.

Batch, real-time, and stream processing

Batch processing is used to process data in batches. It reads data from the input, processes it, and writes it to the output. Apache Hadoop is the most well-known and popular open source implementation of the distributed batch processing system using the MapReduce paradigm. The data is stored in a shared and distributed file system, called **Hadoop Distributed File System** (**HDFS**), and divided into splits, which are the logical data divisions for MapReduce processing.

To process these splits using the MapReduce paradigm, the map task reads the splits and passes all of its key/value pairs to a map function, and writes the results to intermediate files. After the map phase is completed, the reducer reads intermediate files sent through the shuffle process and passes them to the reduce function. Finally, the reduce task writes results to the final output files. The advantages of the MapReduce model include making distributed programming easier, near-linear speed-up, good scalability, as well as fault tolerance. The disadvantage of this batch processing model is being unable to execute recursive or iterative jobs. In addition, the obvious batch behavior is that all input must be ready by map before the reduce job starts, which makes MapReduce unsuitable for online and stream-processing use cases.

Real-time processing is used to process data and get the result almost immediately. This concept in the area of real-time `ad hoc` queries over big data was first implemented in Dremel by Google. It uses a novel columnar storage format for nested structures with fast index and scalable aggregation algorithms for computing query results in parallel instead of batch sequences. These two techniques are the major characters for real-time processing and are used by similar implementations, such as Impala (`https://impala.apache.org/`), Presto (`https://prestodb.io/`), and Drill (`https://drill.apache.org/`), powered by the columnar storage data format, such as Parquet (`https://parquet.apache.org/`), ORC (`https://orc.apache.org/`), CarbonData (`https://carbondata.apache.org/`), and Arrow (`https://arrow.apache.org/`). On the other hand, in-memory computing no doubt offers faster solutions for real-time processing. In-memory computing offers very high bandwidth, which is more than 10 gigabytes/second, compared to a hard disk's 200 megabytes/second. Also, the latency is comparatively lower, nanoseconds versus milliseconds, compared to hard disks. With the price of RAM getting lower and lower each day, in-memory computing is more affordable as a real-time solution, such as Apache Spark (`https://spark.apache.org/`), which is a popular open source implementation of in-memory computing. Spark can be easily integrated with Hadoop, and its in-memory data structure **Resilient Distributed Dataset** (**RDD**) can be generated from data sources, such as HDFS and HBase, for efficient caching.

Stream processing is used to continuously process and act on the live stream data to get a result. In stream processing, there are two commonly used general-purpose stream processing frameworks: Storm (`https://storm.apache.org/`) and Flink (`https://flink.apache.org/`). Both frameworks run on the **Java Virtual Machine** (**JVM**) and both process keyed streams. In terms of the programming model, Storm gives you the basic tools to build a framework, while Flink gives you a well-defined and easily used framework. In addition, Samza (`http://samza.apache.org/`) and Kafka Stream (`https://kafka.apache.org/documentation/streams/`) leverage Kafka for both message-caching and transformation. Recently, Spark also provides a type of stream processing in terms of its innovative continuous-processing mode.

Overview of the Hadoop ecosystem

Hadoop was first released by Apache in 2011 as Version 1.0.0, which only contained HDFS and MapReduce. Hadoop was designed as both a computing (MapReduce) and storage (HDFS) platform from the very beginning. With the increasing need for big data analysis, Hadoop attracts lots of other software to resolve big data questions and merges into a Hadoop-centric big data ecosystem. The following diagram gives a brief overview of the Hadoop big data ecosystem in Apache stack:

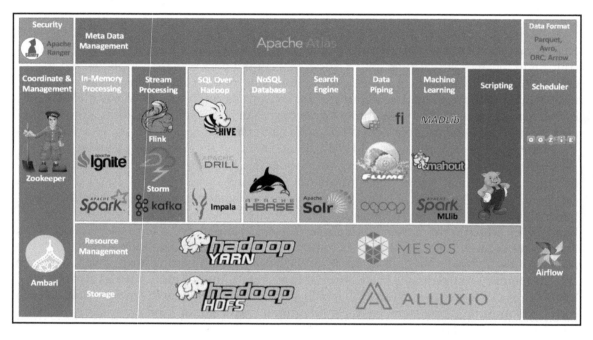

Apache Hadoop ecosystem

In the current Hadoop ecosystem, **HDFS** is still the major option when using hard disk storage, and **Alluxio** provides virtually distributed memory alternatives. On top of HDFS, the Parquet, Avro, and ORC data formats could be used along with a snappy compression algorithm for computing and storage optimization. **Yarn**, as the first Hadoop general-purpose resource manager, is designed for better resource management and scalability. **Spark** and **Ignite**, as in-memory computing engines, are able to run on Yarn to work with Hadoop closely, too.

On the other hand, **Kafka, Flink,** and **Storm** are dominating stream processing. **HBase** is a leading NoSQL database, especially on Hadoop clusters. For machine learning, it comes to **Spark MLlib** and **Madlib** along with a new **Mahout. Sqoop** is still one of the leading tools for exchanging data between Hadoop and relational databases. **Flume** is a matured, distributed, and reliable log-collecting tool to move or collect data to HDFS. **Impala** and **Drill** are able to launch interactive SQL queries directly against the data on Hadoop. In addition, Hive over **Spark/Tez** along with **Live Long And Process** (**LLAP**) offers users the ability to run a query in long-lived processes on different computing frameworks, rather than MapReduce, with in-memory data caching. As a result, **Hive** is playing more important roles in the ecosystem than ever. We are also glad to see that **Ambari** as a new generation of cluster-management tools provides more powerful cluster management and coordination in addition to **Zookeeper.** For scheduling and workflow management, we can either use **Airflow** or **Oozie.** Finally, we have an open source governance and metadata service come into the picture, **Altas,** which empowers the compliance and lineage of big data in the ecosystem.

Hive overview

Hive is a standard for SQL queries over petabytes of data in Hadoop. It provides SQL-like access to data in HDFS, enabling Hadoop to be used as a data warehouse. The **Hive Query Language** (**HQL**) has similar semantics and functions as standard SQL in the relational database, so that experienced database analysts can easily get their hands on it. Hive's query language can run on different computing engines, such as MapReduce, Tez, and Spark.

Hive's metadata structure provides a high-level, table-like structure on top of HDFS. It supports three main data structures, tables, partitions, and buckets. The tables correspond to HDFS directories and can be divided into partitions, where data files can be divided into buckets. Hive's metadata structure is usually the Schema of the Schema-on-Read concept on Hadoop, which means you do not have to define the schema in Hive before you store data in HDFS. Applying Hive metadata after storing data brings more flexibility and efficiency to your data work. The popularity of Hive's metadata makes it the *de facto* way to describe big data and is used by many tools in the big data ecosystem.

The following diagram is the architecture view of Hive in the Hadoop ecosystem. The Hive metadata store (also called the metastore) can use either embedded, local, or remote databases. The thrift server is built on Apache Thrift Server technology. With its latest version 2, hiveserver2 is able to handle multiple concurrent clients, support Kerberos, LDAP, and custom pluggable authentication, and provide better options for JDBC and ODBC clients, especially for metadata access.

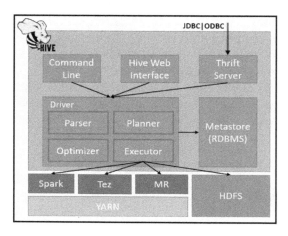

Hive architecture

Here are some highlights of Hive that we can keep in mind moving forward:

- Hive provides a simple and optimized query model with less coding than MapReduce
- HQL and SQL have a similar syntax
- Hive's query response time is typically much faster than others on the same volume of big datasets
- Hive supports running on different computing frameworks
- Hive supports ad hoc querying data on HDFS and HBase
- Hive supports user-defined java/scala functions, scripts, and procedure languages to extend its functionality
- Matured JDBC and ODBC drivers allow many applications to pull Hive data for seamless reporting
- Hive allows users to read data in arbitrary formats, using SerDes and Input/Output formats

- Hive is a stable and reliable batch-processing tool, which is production-ready for a long time
- Hive has a well-defined architecture for metadata management, authentication, and query optimizations
- There is a big community of practitioners and developers working on and using Hive

Summary

After going through this chapter, we are now able to understand when and why to use big data instead of a traditional relational database. We also learned about the difference between batch processing, real-time processing, and stream processing. We are now familiar with the Hadoop ecosystem, especially Hive. We have traveled back in time and brushed through the history of databases, data warehouse, and big data. We also explored some big data terms, the Hadoop ecosystem, the Hive architecture, and the advantage of using Hive.

In the next chapter, we will practice installing Hive and review all the tools needed to start using Hive in the command-line environment.

2

Setting Up the Hive Environment

This chapter will introduce how to install and set up the Hive environment in the cluster and cloud. It also covers the usage of basic Hive commands and the Hive integrated-development environment.

In this chapter, we will cover the following topics:

- Installing Hive from Apache
- Installing Hive from vendors
- Using Hive in the cloud
- Using the Hive command
- Using the Hive IDE

Installing Hive from Apache

To introduce the Hive installation, we will use Hive version 2.3.3 as an example. The pre-installation requirements for this installation are as follows:

- JDK 1.8
- Hadoop 2.x.y
- Ubuntu 16.04/CentOS 7

Since we focus on Hive in this book, the installation steps for Java and Hadoop are not provided here. For steps on installing them, please refer to `https://www.java.com/en/download/help/download_options.xml` and `http://hadoop.apache.org/docs/current/hadoop-project-dist/hadoop-common/ClusterSetup.html`.

The following steps describe how to install Apache Hive in the command-line environment:

1. Download Hive from Apache Hive and unpack it:

```
$cd /opt
$wget https://archive.apache.org/dist/hive/hive-2.3.3/apache-
hive-2.3.3-bin.tar.gz
$tar -zxvf apache-hive-2.3.3-bin.tar.gz
$ln -sfn /opt/apache-hive-2.3.3 /opt/hive
```

2. Add the necessary system path variables in the ~/.profile or ~/.bashrc file:

```
export HADOOP_HOME=/opt/hadoop
export HADOOP_CONF_DIR=/opt/hadoop/conf
export HIVE_HOME=/opt/hive
export HIVE_CONF_DIR=/opt/hive/conf
export PATH=$PATH:$HIVE_HOME/bin:$HADOOP_HOME/
bin:$HADOOP_HOME/sbin
```

3. Enable the settings immediately:

```
$source ~/.profile
```

4. Create the configuration files:

```
$cd /opt/hive/conf
$cp hive-default.xml.template hive-site.xml
$cp hive-exec-log4j.properties.template hive-exec-
log4j.properties
$cp hive-log4j.properties.template hive-log4j.properties
```

5. Modify `$HIVE_HOME/conf/hive-site.xml`, which has some important parameters to set:

   - `hive.metastore.warehourse.dir`: This is the path to the Hive warehouse location. By default, it is at `/user/hive/warehouse`.
   - `hive.exec.scratchdir`: This is the temporary data file location. By default, it is at `/tmp/hive-${user.name}`.

By default, Hive uses the Derby (http://db.apache.org/derby/) database as the metadata store. It can also use other relational databases, such as Oracle, PostgreSQL, or MySQL, as the metastore. To configure the metastore on other databases, the following parameters should be configured in hive-site.xml:

- javax.jdo.option.ConnectionURL: This is the JDBC URL database
- javax.jdo.option.ConnectionDriverName: This is the JDBC driver class name
- javax.jdo.option.ConnectionUserName: This is the username used to access the database
- javax.jdo.option.ConnectionPassword: This is the password used to access the database

The following is a sample setting using MySQL as the metastore database:

```xml
<property>
  <name>javax.jdo.option.ConnectionURL</name>
  <value>jdbc:mysql://localhost/metastore?createDatabaseIfNotExist=true
  </value>
  <description>JDBC connect string for a JDBC metastore</description>
</property>
<property>
  <name>javax.jdo.option.ConnectionDriverName</name>
  <value>com.mysql.jdbc.Driver</value>
  <description>Driver class name for a JDBC metastore</description>
</property>
<property>
  <name>javax.jdo.option.ConnectionUserName</name>
  <value>hive</value>
  <description>username to use against metastore database</description>
</property>
<property>
  <name>javax.jdo.option.ConnectionPassword</name>
  <value>mypassword</value>
  <description>password to use against metastore database</description>
</property>
<property>
  <name>hive.metastore.uris</name>
  <value>thrift://localhost:9083</value>
  <description>By specify this we do not use local mode of
metastore</description>
</property>
```

6. Make sure that the MySQL JDBC driver is available at `$HIVE_HOME/lib`:

```
$ln -sfn /usr/share/java/mysql-connector-java.jar
/opt/hive/lib/mysql-connector-java.jar
```

 The difference between using default Derby or configured relational databases as the metastore is that the configured relational database offers a shared service so that all hive users can see the same metadata set. However, the default metastore setting creates the metastore under the folder of the current user, so it is only visible to this user. In the real production environment, it always configures an external relational database as the Hive metastore.

7. Create the Hive `metastore` table in the database with proper permission, and initialize the schema with `schematool`:

```
$mysql -u root --password="mypassword" -f \
-e "DROP DATABASE IF EXISTS metastore; CREATE DATABASE IF NOT
EXISTS metastore;"
$mysql -u root --password="mypassword" \
-e "GRANT ALL PRIVILEGES ON metastore.* TO 'hive'@'localhost'
IDENTIFIED BY 'mypassword'; FLUSH PRIVILEGES;"
$schematool -dbType mysql -initSchema
```

8. Since Hive runs on Hadoop, first start the hdfs and yarn services, then the `metastore` and `hiveserver2` services:

```
$start-dfs.sh
$start-yarn.sh
$hive --service metastore 1>> /tmp/meta.log 2>> /tmp/meta.log &
$hive --service hiveserver2 1>> /tmp/hs2.log 2>> /tmp/hs2.log &
```

9. Connect Hive with either the `hive` or `beeline` command to verify that the installation is successful:

```
$hive
$beeline -u "jdbc:hive2://localhost:10000"
```

Installing Hive from vendors

Right now, many companies, such as Cloudera and Hortonworks, have packaged the Hadoop ecosystem and management tools into an easily manageable enterprise distribution. Each company takes a slightly different strategy, but the consensus for all of these packages is to make the Hadoop ecosystem easier and more stable for enterprise usage. For example, we can easily install Hive with the Hadoop management tools, such as Cloudera Manager (`https://www.cloudera.com/products/product-components/cloudera-manager.html`) or Ambari (`https://ambari.apache.org/`), which are packed in vendor distributions. Once the management tool is installed and started, we can add the Hive service to the Hadoop cluster with the following steps:

1. Log in to the Cloudera Manager/Ambari and click the **Add a Service** option to enter the **Add Service Wizard**

2. Choose the service to install, such as **hive**

3. Choose the proper hosts for `hiveserver2`, `metastore server`, `WebHCat server`, and so on

4. Configure the `metastore server` database connections as well as other necessary configurations

5. Review and confirm the installation

For practice, we can import the vendors quick-start sandbox (`https://hortonworks.com/products/sandbox/` or `https://www.cloudera.com/downloads/quickstart_vms.html`), which has commonly-used Hadoop ecosystem tools pre-installed. In addition, an automatic and optimized Hadoop environment provision virtual machine is also available (`https://github.com/datafibers/lab_env`) to install on computers with less RAM.

Using Hive in the cloud

Right now, all major cloud service providers, such as Amazon, Microsoft, and Google, offer matured Hadoop and Hive as services in the cloud. Using the cloud version of Hive is very convenient. It requires almost no installation and setup. Amazon EMR (`http://aws.amazon.com/elasticmapreduce/`) is the earliest Hadoop service in the cloud. However, it is not a pure open source version since it is customized to run only on **Amazon Web Services** (**AWS**). Hadoop enterprise service and distribution providers, such as Cloudera and Hortonworks, also provide tools to easily deploy their own distributions on different public or private clouds. Cloudera Director (`http://www.cloudera.com/content/cloudera/en/products-and-services/director.html`) and Cloudbreak (`https://hortonworks.com/open-source/cloudbreak/`), open up Hadoop deployments in the cloud through a simple, self-service interface, and are fully supported on AWS, Windows Azure, Google Cloud Platform, and OpenStack. Although Hadoop was first built on Linux, Hortonworks and Microsoft have already partnered to bring Hadoop to the Windows-based platform and cloud successfully. The consensus among all the Hadoop cloud service providers here is to allow enterprises to provision highly available, flexible, highly secure, easily manageable, and governable Hadoop clusters with less effort and little cost.

Using the Hive command

Hive first started with `hiveserver1`. However, this version of Hive server was not very stable. It sometimes suspended or blocked the client's connection quietly. Since v0.11.0, Hive has included a new thrift server called `hivesever2` to replace `hiveserver1`. `hiveserver2` has an enhanced server designed for multiple client concurrency and improved authentication. It also recommends using `beeline` as the major Hive command-line interface instead of the `hive` command. The primary difference between the two versions of servers is how the clients connect to them. `hive` is an Apache-Thrift-based client, and `beeline` is a JDBC client. The `hive` command directly connects to the Hive drivers, so we need to install the Hive library on the client. However, `beeline` connects to `hiveserver2` through JDBC connections without installing Hive libraries on the client. That means we can run `beeline` remotely from outside the cluster. For more usage of `hiveserver2` and its API access, refer to `https://cwiki.apache.org/confluence/display/Hive/HiveServer2+Clients`.

The following two tables list the commonly-used commands in different command modes considering different user preferences:

Purpose	hiveserver2 - beeline	hiveserver1 - hive
Connect server	`beeline -u <jdbc_url>`	`hive -h <hostname> -p <port>`
Help	`beeline -h`	`hive -H`

Run query	`beeline -e "hql query"`
	`beeline -f hql_query_file.hql`
	`beeline -i hql_init_file.hql`
		`hive -e "hql query"`
		`hive -f hql_query_file.hql`
		`hive -i hql_init_file.hql`

Set variable	`beeline --hivevar` `var_name=var_value`	`hive --hivevar var_name=var_value`

Purpose	hiveserver2 - beeline	hiveserver1 - hive
Enter mode	`beeline`	`hive`
Connect server	`!connect <jdbc_url>`	N/A
List tables	`!table` `show tables; --also support`	`show tables;`
List columns	`!column table_name` `desc table_name;`	`desc table_name;`
Run query	`select * from table_name;`	`select * from table_name;`
Save result	`!record result_file.dat` `!record`	N/A
Run shell cmd	`!sh ls`	`!ls;`
Run dfs cmd	`dfs -ls;`	`dfs -ls;`
Run hql file	`!run hql_query_file.hql`	`source hql_query_file.hql;`
Quit mode	`!quit`	`quit;`

In addition, Hive configuration settings and properties can be accessed and overwritten by the SET keyword in the interactive mode. For more details, refer to the Apache Hive wiki at `https://cwiki.apache.org/confluence/display/Hive/Configuration+Properties`.

For beeline, ; is not needed after the command that starts with !. Both commands do not support running a pasted query with <tab> inside, because <tab> is used for auto-complete by default in the environment. Alternatively, running the query from files has no such issues. In interactive mode, we can use the keyboard's up and down arrow keys to retrieve the previous commands. The `!history` command can be used in beeline to show the command's history. In addition, the `dfs` command may be disabled in beeline for permissions control in some Hadoop distributions. Both commands support variable substitution, which refers to `https://cwiki.apache.org/confluence/display/Hive/LanguageManual+VariableSubstitution`.

Using the Hive IDE

Besides the command-line interface, there are other **Integrated Development Environment** (**IDE**) tools available to support Hive. One of the best is **Oracle SQL Developer**, which leverages the powerful functionalities of the Oracle IDE and is totally free to use. Since Oracle SQL Developer supports general JDBC connections, it is quite convenient to switch between Hive and other JDBC-supported databases in the same IDE. Oracle SQL Developer has supported Hive since v4.0.3. Configuring it to work with Hive is quite straightforward:

1. Download Oracle SQL Developer (`http://www.oracle.com/technetwork/developer-tools/sql-developer/downloads/index.html`).

2. Download the Hive JDBC drivers (`https://www.cloudera.com/downloads/connectors/hive/jdbc.html`).

3. Unzip the driver file to a local directory.

4. Start Oracle SQL Developer and navigate to **Preferences** | **Database** | **Third Party JDBC Drivers**.

5. Add all of the JAR files contained in the unzipped directory to the window, as shown in the following screenshot:

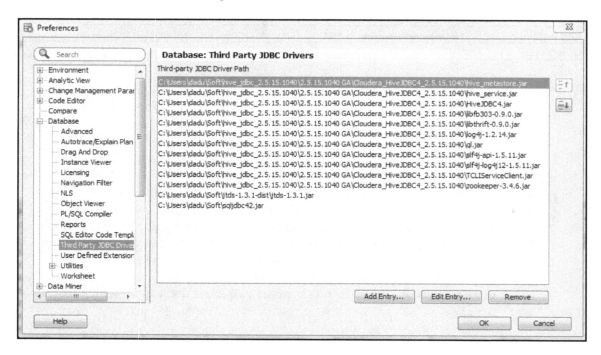

6. Click on the **OK** button and restart Oracle SQL Developer.
7. Create a new connection in the **Hive** tab, giving the proper **Connection Name**, **Username**, **Password**, **Host name** (`hiveserver2 hostname`), **Port**, and **Database**. Then, click on the **Add** and **Connect** buttons to connect to Hive:

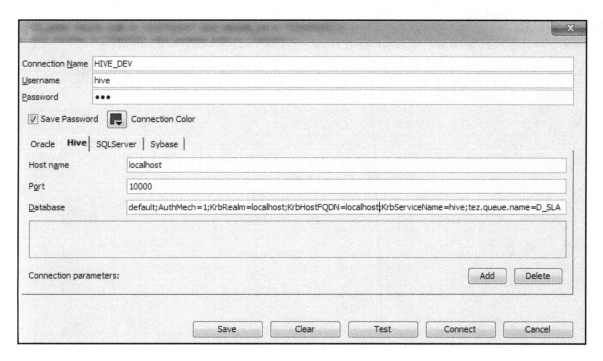

In Oracle SQL Developer, we can run all Hive interactive commands and HQL queries. We can also leverage the wizard of the tool to browse or export data in the Hive tables. Besides Oracle SQL Developer, other database IDEs, such as DBVisualizer (`https://www.dbvis.com/`) or SQuirrel SQL Client (`http://squirrel-sql.sourceforge.net/`), can also use the ODBC or JDBC driver to connect to Hive. Hive also has its own built-in web IDE, Hive Web Interface. However, it is not powerful and seldom used. Instead, both Ambari Hive View and Hue (`http://gethue.com/`) are popular, user-friendly, and powerful web IDEs for the Hadoop and Hive ecosystem. There are more details about using these IDEs in `Chapter 10`, *Working with Other Tools*.

Summary

In this chapter, we learned how to set up Hive in different environments. We also looked into a few examples of using Hive commands in both the command-line and the interactive mode for `beeline` and `hive`. Since it is quite productive to use IDE with Hive, we walked through the setup of Oracle SQL Developer for Hive. Now that you've finished this chapter, you should be able to set up your own Hive environment locally and use Hive.

In the next chapter, we will dive into the details of Hive's data definition languages.

Data Definition and Description

3

This chapter introduces the basic data types, data definition language, and schema in Hive to describe data. It also covers best practices to describe data correctly and effectively by using internal or external tables, partitions, buckets, and views. In this chapter, we will cover the following topics:

- Understanding data types
- Data type conversions
- Data definition language
- Databases
- Tables
- Partitions
- Buckets
- Views

Understanding data types

Hive data types are categorized into two types: primitive and complex. String and Int are the most useful primitive types, which are supported by most HQL functions. The details of primitive types are as follows:

ay contain a set of any type of fields. Complex types allow the nesting of types. The details of complex types a

Primitive type	Description	Example
TINYINT	It has 1 byte, from −128 to 127. The postfix is Y. It is used as a small range of numbers.	10Y
SMALLINT	It has 2 bytes, from −32,768 to 32,767. The postfix is S. It is used as a regular descriptive number.	10S

Primitive type	Description	Example
INT	It has 4 bytes, from $-2,147,483,648$ to $2,147,483,647$.	10
BIGINT	It has 8 bytes, from $-9,223,372,036,854,775,808$ to $9,223,372,036,854,775,807$. The postfix is L.	100L
FLOAT	This is a 4 byte single-precision floating-point number, from $1.40129846432481707e^{-45}$ to $3.40282346638528860e^{+38}$ (positive or negative). Scientific notation is not yet supported. It stores very close approximations of numeric values.	1.2345679
DOUBLE	This is an 8 byte double-precision floating-point number, from $4.94065645841246544e^{-324d}$ to $1.79769313486231570e^{+308d}$ (positive or negative). Scientific notation is not yet supported. It stores very close approximations of numeric values.	1.2345678901234567
BINARY	This was introduced in Hive 0.8.0 and only supports CAST to STRING and vice versa.	1011
BOOLEAN	This is a TRUE or FALSE value.	TRUE
STRING	This includes characters expressed with either single quotes (') or double quotes ("). Hive uses C-style escaping within the strings. The max size is around 2 G.	'Books' or "Books"
CHAR	This is available starting with Hive 0.13.0. Most UDF will work for this type after Hive 0.14.0. The maximum length is fixed at 255.	'US' or "US"
VARCHAR	This is available starting with Hive 0.12.0. Most UDF will work for this type after Hive 0.14.0. The maximum length is fixed at 65,355. If a string value being converted/assigned to a varchar value exceeds the length specified, the string is silently truncated.	'Books' or "Books"
DATE	This describes a specific year, month, and day in the format of YYYY-MM-DD. It is available starting with Hive 0.12.0. The range of dates is from 0000-01-01 to 9999-12-31.	2013-01-01
TIMESTAMP	This describes a specific year, month, day, hour, minute, second, and millisecond in the format of YYYY-MM-DD HH:MM:SS[.fff...]. It is available starting with Hive 0.8.0.	2013-01-01 12:00:01.345

Hive has three main complex types: ARRAY, MAP, and STRUCT. These data types are built on top of the primitive data types. ARRAY and MAP are similar to that in Java. STRUCT is a record type, which may contain a set of any type of fields. Complex types allow the nesting of types. The details of complex types are as follows:

Complex type	Description	Example
ARRAY	This is a list of items of the same type, such as [val1, val2, and so on]. You can access the value using `array_name[index]`, for example, `fruit[0]="apple"`. Index starts from 0.	`["apple","orange","mango"]`
MAP	This is a set of key-value pairs, such as {key1, val1, key2, val2, and so on}. You can access the value using `map_name[key]` for example, `fruit[1]="apple"`.	`{1: "apple",2: "orange"}`
STRUCT	This is a user-defined structure of any type of field, such as {val1, val2, val3, and so on}. By default, STRUCT field names will be col1, col2, and so on. You can access the value using `structs_name.column_name`, for example, `fruit.col1=1`.	`{1, "apple"}`
NAMED STRUCT	This is a user-defined structure of any number of typed fields, such as {name1, val1, name2, val2, and so on}. You can access the value using `structs_name.column_name`, for example, `fruit.apple="gala"`.	`{"apple":"gala","weight kg":1}`
UNION	This is a structure that has exactly any one of the specified data types. It is available starting with Hive 0.7.0. It is not commonly used.	`{2:["apple","orange"]}`

> For MAP, the type of keys and values are unified. However, STRUCT is more flexible. STRUCT is more like a table, whereas MAP is more like an ARRAY with a customized index.

The following is a short exercise for all the commonly-used data types. The details of the CREATE, LOAD, and SELECT statements will be introduced in later chapters. Let's take a look at the exercise:

1. Prepare the data as follows:

```
$vi employee.txt
Michael|Montreal,Toronto|Male,30|DB:80|Product:Developer^DLead
Will|Montreal|Male,35|Perl:85|Product:Lead,Test:Lead
Shelley|New York|Female,27|Python:80|Test:Lead,COE:Architect
Lucy|Vancouver|Female,57|Sales:89,HR:94|Sales:Lead
```

2. Log in to beeline with the JDBC URL:

```
$beeline -u "jdbc:hive2://localhost:10000/default"
```

3. Create a table using various data types (> indicates the beeline interactive mode):

```
> CREATE TABLE employee (
>    name STRING,
>    work_place ARRAY<STRING>,
>    gender_age STRUCT<gender:STRING,age:INT>,
>    skills_score MAP<STRING,INT>,
>    depart_title MAP<STRING,ARRAY<STRING>>
> )
> ROW FORMAT DELIMITED
> FIELDS TERMINATED BY '|'
> COLLECTION ITEMS TERMINATED BY ','
> MAP KEYS TERMINATED BY ':'
> STORED AS TEXTFILE;
No rows affected (0.149 seconds)
```

4. Verify that the table has been created:

```
> !table employee
+-----------+--------------+-------------+-----------------+----------+
|TABLE_CAT|TABLE_SCHEMA| TABLE_NAME  |  TABLE_TYPE   | REMARKS |
+-----------+--------------+-------------+-----------------+----------+
|          |default      | employee    | MANAGED_TABLE|          |
+-----------+--------------+-------------+-----------------+----------+
> !column employee
--------------+--------------+---------------+--------------------+
| TABLE_SCHEM | TABLE_NAME  | COLUMN_NAME | TYPE_NAME          |
+-------------+--------------+---------------+--------------------+
| default     | employee    | name        | STRING             |
| default     | employee    | work_place  | array<string>      |
| default     | employee    | gender_age  |
struct<gender:string,age:int>|
| default     | employee    | skills_score| map<string,int>    |
| default     | employee    | depart_title|
map<string,array<string>>    |
+-------------+--------------+---------------+--------------------+
```

5. Load data into the table:

```
> LOAD DATA INPATH '/tmp/hivedemo/data/employee.txt'
> OVERWRITE INTO TABLE employee;
No rows affected (1.023 seconds)
```

6. Query the whole array and each array element in the table:

```
> SELECT work_place FROM employee;
+-----------------------+
|       work_place      |
+-----------------------+
| [Montreal, Toronto]   |
| [Montreal]            |
| [New York]            |
| [Vancouver]           |
+-----------------------+
4 rows selected (27.231 seconds)

> SELECT
> work_place[0] as col_1, work_place[1] as col_2,
> work_place[2] as col_3
> FROM employee;
+-------------+-----------+---------+
|   col_1     |   col_2   |  col_3  |
+-------------+-----------+---------+
| Montreal    | Toronto   |         |
| Montreal    |           |         |
| New York    |           |         |
| Vancouver   |           |         |
-------------+-----------+---------+
4 rows selected (24.689 seconds)
```

7. Query the whole struct and each struct attribute in the table:

```
> SELECT gender_age FROM employee;
+--------------------+
|     gender_age     |
+--------------------+
| [Male, 30]         |
| [Male, 35]         |
| [Female, 27]       |
| [Female, 57]       |
+--------------------+
4 rows selected (28.91 seconds)

> SELECT gender_age.gender, gender_age.age FROM employee;
+-------------+------+
```

```
|   gender    |  age  |
+------------+------+
| Male       | 30    |
| Male       | 35    |
| Female     | 27    |
| Female     | 57    |
+------------+------+
4 rows selected (26.663 seconds)
```

8. Query the whole map and each map element in the table:

```
> SELECT skills_score FROM employee;
+--------------------+
|    skills_score    |
+--------------------+
| {DB=80}            |
| {Perl=85}          |
| {Python=80}        |
| {Sales=89, HR=94}  |
+--------------------+
4 rows selected (32.659 seconds)

> SELECT
> name, skills_score['DB'] as DB, skills_score['Perl'] as Perl,
> skills_score['Python'] as Python,
> skills_score['Sales'] as Sales,
> skills_score['HR'] as HR
> FROM employee;
+----------+-----+-------+---------+--------+-----+
|  name    | db  | perl  | python  | sales  | hr  |
+----------+-----+-------+---------+--------+-----+
| Michael  | 80  |       |         |        |     |
| Will     |     | 85    |         |        |     |
| Shelley  |     |       | 80      |        |     |
| Lucy     |     |       |         | 89     | 94  |
+----------+-----+-------+---------+--------+-----+
4 rows selected (24.669 seconds)
```

 Note that the column name shown in the result or in the hive statement is not case sensitive. It is always shown in lowercase letters.

9. Query the composite type in the table:

```
> SELECT depart_title FROM employee;
+----------------------------------+
|           depart_title           |
+----------------------------------+
| {Product=[Developer, Lead]}      |
| {Test=[Lead], Product=[Lead]}    |
| {Test=[Lead], COE=[Architect]}   |
| {Sales=[Lead]}                   |
+----------------------------------+
4 rows selected (30.583 seconds)

> SELECT
> name, depart_title['Product'] as Product, depart_title['Test']
as Test,
> depart_title['COE'] as COE, depart_title['Sales'] as Sales
> FROM employee;
+---------+--------------------+---------+-------------+------+
|  name   |      product       |  test   |     coe     |sales |
+---------+--------------------+---------+-------------+------+
| Michael| [Developer, Lead]  |         |             |      |
| Will   | [Lead]             | [Lead]  |             |      |
| Shelley|                    | [Lead]  | [Architect] |      |
| Lucy   |                    |         |             |[Lead]|
+---------+--------------------+---------+-------------+------+
4 rows selected (26.641 seconds)

> SELECT
> name, depart_title['Product'][0] as product_col0,
> depart_title['Test'][0] as test_col0
> FROM employee;
+----------+---------------+------------+
|   name   | product_col0  | test_col0  |
+----------+---------------+------------+
| Michael  | Developer     |            |
| Will     | Lead          | Lead       |
| Shelley  |               | Lead       |
| Lucy     |               |            |
+----------+---------------+------------+
4 rows selected (26.659 seconds)
```

The default delimiters in table-creation DDL are as follows:

- **Row Delimiter**: This can be used with *Ctrl + A* or ^A (use \001 when creating the table)
- **Collection Item Delimiter**: This can be used with *Ctrl + B* or ^B (\002)
- **Map Key Delimiter**: This can be used with *Ctrl + C* or ^C (\003)

If the delimiter is overridden during the table creation, it only works when used in the flat structure. This is still a limitation in Hive described in Apache Jira Hive-365 (https://issues.apache.org/jira/browse/HIVE-365). For nested types, the level of nesting determines the delimiter. Using ARRAY of ARRAY as an example, the delimiters for the outer ARRAY, as expected, are *Ctrl + B* characters, but the inner ARRAY delimiter becomes *Ctrl + C* characters, which is the next delimiter in the list. In the preceding example, the depart_title column, which is a MAP of ARRAY, the MAP key delimiter is *Ctrl + C*, and the ARRAY delimiter is *Ctrl + D*.

Data type conversions

Similar to SQL, HQL supports both implicit and explicit type conversion. Primitive-type conversion from a narrow to a wider type is known as implicit conversion. However, the reverse conversion is not allowed. All the integral numeric types, FLOAT, and STRING can be implicitly converted to DOUBLE, and TINYINT, SMALLINT, and INT can all be converted to FLOAT. BOOLEAN types cannot be converted to any other type. There is a data type cross-table describing the allowed implicit conversion between every two types, which can be found at https://cwiki.apache.org/confluence/display/Hive/LanguageManual+Types. Explicit-type conversion uses the CAST function with the CAST(value as TYPE) syntax. For example, CAST('100' as INT) will convert the 100 string to the 100 integer value. If the cast fails, such as CAST('INT' as INT), the function returns NULL.

In addition, the BINARY type can only first cast to STRING, then cast from STRING to other types if needed.

Data Definition Language

Hive's **Data Definition Language** (**DDL**) is a subset of HQL statements that describe the Hive data structure by creating, deleting, or altering schema objects such as databases, tables, views, partitions, and buckets. Most DDL statements start with the CREATE, DROP, or ALTER keywords. The syntax of HQL DDL is very similar to SQL DDL. In the next section, we'll focus on the details of HQL DDL.

 HQL uses -- before a single line of characters as comments, and it does not support multiline comments until v2.3.0. After v2.3.0, we can use bracketed single or multiline comments between /* and */.

Database

The database in Hive describes a collection of tables that are used for a similar purpose or belong to the same groups. If the database is not specified, the default database is used and uses /user/hive/warehouse in HDFS as its root directory. This path is configurable by the hive.metastore.warehouse.dir property in hive-site.xml. Whenever a new database is created, Hive creates a new directory for each database under /user/hive/warehouse. For example, the myhivebook database is located at /user/hive/datawarehouse/myhivebook.db. In addition, DATABASE has a name alias, **SCHEMA**, meaning they are the same thing in HQL. The following is the major DDL for databases operations:

1. Create the database/schema if it doesn't exist:

   ```
   > CREATE DATABASE myhivebook;
   > CREATE SCHEMA IF NOT EXISTS myhivebook;
   ```

2. Create the database with the location, comments, and metadata information:

   ```
   > CREATE DATABASE IF NOT EXISTS myhivebook
   > COMMENT 'hive database demo'
   > LOCATION '/hdfs/directory'
   > WITH DBPROPERTIES ('creator'='dayongd','date'='2018-05-01');

   -- To show the DDL use show create database since v2.1.0
   > SHOW CREATE DATABASE default;
   +----------------------------------------------------+
   | createdb_stmt                                      |
   +----------------------------------------------------+
   ```

```
| CREATE DATABASE `default`                      |
| COMMENT                                        |
| 'Default Hive database'                        |
| LOCATION                                       |
| 'hdfs://localhost:9000/user/hive/warehouse'    |
+------------------------------------------------+
```

3. Show and describe the database with wildcards:

```
> SHOW DATABASES;
+-----------------+
| database_name   |
+-----------------+
| default         |
+-----------------+
1 row selected (1.7 seconds)

> SHOW DATABASES LIKE 'my.*';
> DESCRIBE DATABASE default;
+--------+---------------------+-------------------------------+
|db_name|      comment        |            location           |
+--------+---------------------+-------------------------------+
|default|Default Hive database | hdfs://localhost:9000
                                  /user/hive/warehouse          |
+--------+---------------------+-------------------------------+
1 row selected (1.352 seconds)
```

4. Switch to use one database or directly qualify the table name with the database name:

```
> USE myhivebook;
> --SELECT * FROM myhivebook.table_name;
```

5. Show the current database:

```
> SELECT current_database();
+-----------+
| _c0       |
+-----------+
| default   |
+-----------+
1 row selected (0.218 seconds)
```

6. Drop the database:

```
> DROP DATABASE IF EXISTS myhivebook;--failed when database is
not empty
> DROP DATABASE IF EXISTS myhivebook CASCADE;--drop database and
tables
```

 Hive databases/tables are directories/subdirectories in HDFS. In order to remove the database directory, we need to remove the subdirectories (for tables) first. By default, the database cannot be dropped if it is not empty, unless the CASCADE option is specified. With this option, it drops all tables in the database automatically before dropping the database.

7. Alter the database properties. The ALTER DATABASE statement can only apply to dbproperties, owner, and location on the database. The other database properties cannot be changed:

```
> ALTER DATABASE myhivebook SET DBPROPERTIES ('edited-
by'='Dayong');
> ALTER DATABASE myhivebook SET OWNER user dayongd;
> ALTER DATABASE myhivebook SET LOCATION '/tmp/data/myhivebook';
```

 Since Hive v2.2.1, the ALTER DATABASE ... SET LOCATION statement can be used to modify the database's location, but it does not move all existing tables/partitions in the current database directory to the newly specified location. It only changes the location for newly added tables after the database is altered. This behavior is analogous to how changing a table-directory does not move existing partitions to a different location.

 The SHOW and DESC (or DESCRIBE) statements in Hive are used to show the definition for most of the objects, such as tables and partitions. The SHOW statement supports a wide range of Hive objects, such as tables, tables' properties, table DDL, index, partitions, columns, functions, locks, roles, configurations, transactions, and compactions. The DESC statement supports a small range of Hive objects, such as databases, tables, views, columns, and partitions. However, the DESC statement is able to provide more detailed information combined with the EXTENDED or FORMATTED keywords. In this book, there is no dedicated section to introduce SHOW and DESC. Instead, we introduce them in line with other HQL through the remaining chapters.

Tables

The concept of a table in Hive is very similar to the table in the relational database. Each table maps to a directory, which is under `/user/hive/warehouse` by default in HDFS. For example, `/user/hive/warehouse/employee` is created for the `employee` table. All the data in the table is stored in this hive user-manageable directory (full permission). This kind of table is called an internal, or managed, table. When data is already stored in HDFS, an external table can be created to describe the data. It is called `external` because the data in the external table is specified in the `LOCATION` property rather than the default warehouse directory. When keeping data in the internal tables, the table fully manages the data in it. When an internal table is dropped, its data is deleted together. However, when an external table is dropped, the data is not deleted. It is quite common to use external tables for source read-only data or sharing the processed data to data consumers giving customized HDFS locations. On the other hand, the internal table is often used as an intermediate table during data processing, since it is quite powerful and flexible when supported by HQL.

Table creation

The following are major DDLs for the internal and external table creation:

1. Show the data file content of `employee.txt`:

```
$ vi /home/hadoop/employee.txt
Michael|Montreal,Toronto|Male,30|DB:80|Product:Developer^DLead
Will|Montreal|Male,35|Perl:85|Product:Lead,Test:Lead
Shelley|New York|Female,27|Python:80|Test:Lead,COE:Architect
Lucy|Vancouver|Female,57|Sales:89,HR:94|Sales:Lead
```

2. Create an internal table and load the data:

```
> CREATE TABLE IF NOT EXISTS employee_internal (
> name STRING COMMENT 'this is optinal column comments',
> work_place ARRAY<STRING>,-- table column names are NOT case
sensitive
> gender_age STRUCT<gender:STRING,age:INT>,
> skills_score MAP<STRING,INT>, -- columns names are lower case
> depart_title MAP<STRING,ARRAY<STRING>>-- No "," for the last
column
> )
```

```
> COMMENT 'This is an internal table'-- This is optional table
comments
> ROW FORMAT DELIMITED
> FIELDS TERMINATED BY '|'        -- Symbol to seperate columns
> COLLECTION ITEMS TERMINATED BY ','-- Seperate collection elements
> MAP KEYS TERMINATED BY ':'    -- Symbol to seperate keys and values
> STORED as TEXTFILE;            -- Table file format
No rows affected (0.149 seconds)

> LOAD DATA INPATH '/tmp/hivedemo/data/employee.txt'
> OVERWRITE INTO TABLE employee_internal;
```

If the folder path does not exist in the LOCATION property, Hive will create that folder. If there is another folder inside it, Hive will NOT report errors when creating the table but querying the table.

3. Create an external table and load the data:

```
> CREATE EXTERNAL TABLE employee_external ( -- Use EXTERNAL keywords
> name string,
> work_place ARRAY<string>,
> gender_age STRUCT<gender:string,age:int>,
> skills_score MAP<string,int>,
> depart_title MAP<STRING,ARRAY<STRING>>
> )
> ROW FORMAT DELIMITED
> FIELDS TERMINATED BY '|'
> COLLECTION ITEMS TERMINATED BY ','
> MAP KEYS TERMINATED BY ':'
> STORED as TEXTFILE
> LOCATION '/user/dayongd/employee'; -- Specify data folder location
No rows affected (1.332 seconds)

> LOAD DATA INPATH '/tmp/hivedemo/data/employee.txt'
> OVERWRITE INTO TABLE employee_external;
```

Since v2.1.0, Hive supports primary and foreign key constraints. However, these constraints are not validated, so the upstream system needs to ensure data integrity before it's loaded into Hive. The Hive constraints may benefit some SQL tools to generate more efficient queries with them, but they are not used very often.

Hive also supports creating temporary tables. A temporary table is only visible to the current user session. It's automatically deleted at the end of the session. The data of the temporary table is stored in the user's scratch directory, such as /tmp/hive-<username>. Therefore, make sure the folder is properly configured or secured when you have sensitive data in temporary tables. Whenever a temporary table has the same name as a permanent table, the temporary table will be chosen rather than the permanent table. A temporary table does not support partitions and indexes. The following are three ways to create temporary tables:

```
> CREATE TEMPORARY TABLE IF NOT EXISTS tmp_emp1 (
> name string,
> work_place ARRAY<string>,
> gender_age STRUCT<gender:string,age:int>,
> skills_score MAP<string,int>,
> depart_title MAP<STRING,ARRAY<STRING>>
> );
No rows affected (0.122 seconds)

> CREATE TEMPORARY TABLE tmp_emp2 as SELECT * FROM tmp_emp1;
> CREATE TEMPORARY TABLE tmp_emp3 like tmp_emp1;
```

Tables can also be created and populated by the results of a query in one statement, called Create-Table-As-Select (**CTAS**). The table created by CTAS is not visible by other users until all the query results are populated. CTAS has the following restrictions:

- The table created cannot be a partitioned table
- The table created cannot be an external table
- The table created cannot be a list-bucketing table

A CTAS statement always triggers a yarn job to populate the data, although the SELECT * statement itself does not trigger any yarn job.

CTAS can also be used with **CTE**, which stands for **C**ommon **T**able **E**xpression. CTE is a temporary result set derived from a simple select query specified in a WITH clause, followed by the SELECT or INSERT statement to build the result set. The CTE is defined only within the execution scope of a single statement. One or more CTEs can be used in a nested or chained way with keywords, such as the SELECT, INSERT, CREATE TABLE AS SELECT, or CREATE VIEW AS SELECT statements. Using CTE of HQL makes the query more concise and clear than writing complex nested queries.

The following are examples using CTAS and CTE for table creation:

1. Create a table with CTAS:

```
> CREATE TABLE ctas_employee as SELECT * FROM employee_external;
No rows affected (1.562 seconds)
```

2. Create a table with both CTAS and CTE:

```
> CREATE TABLE cte_employee as
> WITH r1 as (
> SELECT name FROM r2 WHERE name = 'Michael'
> ),
> r2 as (
> SELECT name FROM employee WHERE gender_age.gender= 'Male'
> ),
> r3 as (
> SELECT name FROM employee WHERE gender_age.gender= 'Female'
> )
> SELECT * FROM r1
> UNION ALL
> SELECT * FROM r3;
No rows affected (61.852 seconds)

> SELECT * FROM cte_employee;
+------------------------------+
| cte_employee.name            |
+------------------------------+
| Michael                      |
| Shelley                      |
| Lucy                         |
+------------------------------+
3 rows selected (0.091 seconds)
```

3. Use CTAS to create an empty table by copying the schema from another table. It is empty because the where condition is false:

```
> CREATE TABLE empty_ctas_employee as
> SELECT * FROM employee_internal WHERE 1=2;
No rows affected (213.356 seconds)
```

4. In another way, we can also use CREATE TABLE LIKE to create an empty table. This is a faster way to copy the table schema since it does not trigger any jobs but only copies metadata:

```
> CREATE TABLE empty_like_employee LIKE employee_internal;
No rows affected (0.115 seconds)
```

Table description

Since we deal with tables most of the time, there are a few useful table-information display commands, as follows:

1. Show tables with regular expression filters:

```
> SHOW TABLES; -- Show all tables in database
> SHOW TABLES '*sam*'; -- Show tables name contains "sam"
> SHOW TABLES '*sam|lily*'; -- Show tables name contains "sam" or
"lily"
```

2. List detailed table information for all tables matching the given regular expression:

```
>SHOW TABLE EXTENDED LIKE 'employee_int*';
OK
tableName:employee_internal
owner:dayongd
location:hdfs://localhost/user/hive/warehouse/employee_internal
inputformat:org.apache.hadoop.mapred.TextInputFormat
outputformat:org.apache.hadoop.hive.ql.io.HiveIgnoreKeyText
OutputFormatcolumns:struct columns { i32 num}
partitioned:false
partitionColumns:
totalNumberFiles:0
totalFileSize:0
maxFileSize:0
minFileSize:0
lastAccessTime:0
lastUpdateTime:1274517075221
```

3. Show table-column information in two ways:

```
> SHOW COLUMNS IN employee_internal;
+---------------+
|     field     |
+---------------+
| name          |
| work_place    |
| gender_age    |
| skills_score  |
| depart_title  |
+---------------+
5 rows selected (0.101 seconds)
```

```
> DESC employee_internal;
+----------------+-------------------------------------+-----------+
| col_name       | data_type                           | comment   |
+----------------+-------------------------------------+-----------+
| name           | string                              |           |
| work_place     | array<string>                       |           |
| gender_age     | struct<gender:string,age:int>       |           |
| skills_score   | map<string,int>                     |           |
| depart_title   | map<string,array<string>>           |           |
+----------------+-------------------------------------+-----------+
5 rows selected (0.127 seconds)
```

4. Show create-table DDL statements for the specified table:

```
> SHOW CREATE TABLE employee_internal;
+----------------------------------------------------------------------+
|                            createtab_stmt                            |
+----------------------------------------------------------------------+
| CREATE TABLE `employee_internal`(                                    |
| `name` string,                                                       |
| `work_place` array<string>,                                          |
| `gender_age` struct<gender:string,age:int>,                          |
| `skills_score` map<string,int>,                                      |
| `depart_title` map<string,array<string>>)                            |
| COMMENT 'this is an internal table'                                   |
| ROW FORMAT SERDE                                                      |
| 'org.apache.hadoop.hive.serde2.lazy.LazySimpleSerDe'                 |
| WITH SERDEPROPERTIES (                                               |
| 'colelction.delim'=',',                                              |
| 'field.delim'='|',                                                   |
| 'mapkey.delim'=':',                                                  |
| 'serialization.format'='|')                                          |
| STORED as INPUTFORMAT                                                 |
| 'org.apache.hadoop.mapred.TextInputFormat'                           |
| OUTPUTFORMAT                                                          |
| 'org.apache.hadoop.hive.ql.io.HiveIgnoreKeyTextOutputFormat'         |
| LOCATION                                                             |
| 'hdfs://localhost:9000/user/hive/warehouse/employee_internal'|
| TBLPROPERTIES (                                                       |
| 'transient_lastDdlTime'='1523108773')                                |
+----------------------------------------------------------------------+
22 rows selected (0.191 seconds)
```

5. Show table properties for the specified table:

```
> SHOW TBLPROPERTIES employee_internal;
+-------------------------+---------------------------+
| prpt_name               | prpt_value                |
```

```
+-----------------------+---------------------------+
| comment               | this is an internal table |
| numFiles              | 1                         |
| numRows               | 0                         |
| rawDataSize           | 0                         |
| totalSize             | 227                       |
| transient_lastDdlTime | 1523108773                |
+-----------------------+---------------------------+
6 rows selected (0.095 seconds)
```

Table cleaning

Sometimes, we may need to clean up the table, either by deleting only the records or the table along with the records. There are two statements in HQL to do such cleaning. One is the DROP TABLE statement, and the other is TRUNCATE TABLE. The drop-table statement on an internal table removes the table completely and moves data to .trash in the current user directory, if the trash setting is configured. The drop-table statement on an external table will only remove the table definition, but keeps data:

```
> DROP TABLE IF EXISTS empty_ctas_employee;
No rows affected (0.283 seconds)
```

On the other hand, the truncate table statement only removes data from the table. The table still exists, but is empty. Note, truncate table can only apply to an internal table:

```
> TRUNCATE TABLE cte_employee; -- Only apply to internal tables
No rows affected (0.093 seconds)
> SELECT name FROM cte_employee; --Other hand, the truncate t
-- Not data left, but empty table exists
+--------------------+
| cte_employee.name  |
+--------------------+
+--------------------+
No rows selected (0.059 seconds)
```

Table alteration

Once a table is created, we can still modify its metadata, such as adding new columns and changing the column's data type. In HQL, we use the ALTER command to modify the table's metadata. However, alter table is not able to update the data accordingly. We should make sure the actual data conforms to the metadata definition manually, otherwise the query will return nothing in expectation.

The following are examples for altering tables in HQL:

1. Rename a table with the `ALTER` statement. This is quite often used as data backup:

```
> ALTER TABLE cte_employee RENAME TO cte_employee_backup;
No rows affected (0.237 seconds)
```

2. Change the table properties with `TBLPROPERTIES`:

```
> ALTER TABLE c_employee SET TBLPROPERTIES
('comment'='New comments');
No rows affected (0.239 seconds)
```

3. Change the table's row format and SerDe (SerDe is introduced in `Chapter 8`, *Extensibility Considerations*) with `SERDEPROPERTIES`:

```
> ALTER TABLE employee_internal SET SERDEPROPERTIES
('field.delim' = '$');
No rows affected (0.148 seconds)
```

4. Change the table's file format with `FILEFORMAT`:

```
> ALTER TABLE c_employee SET FILEFORMAT RCFILE;
No rows affected (0.235 seconds)
```

5. Change the table's location, a full URI of HDFS, with `LOCATION`:

```
> ALTER TABLE c_employee SET LOCATION
'hdfs://localhost:9000/tmp/employee';
No rows affected (0.169 seconds)
```

6. Enable/Disable the table's protection; `NO_DROP` or `OFFLINE`. `NO_DROP` prevents a table from being dropped, while `OFFLINE` prevents data (not metadata) from being queried in a table:

```
> ALTER TABLE c_employee ENABLE NO_DROP;
> ALTER TABLE c_employee DISABLE NO_DROP;
> ALTER TABLE c_employee ENABLE OFFLINE;
> ALTER TABLE c_employee DISABLE OFFLINE;
```

7. Enable concatenation in an `RCFile`, or `ORC` table if it has many small files:

```
> ALTER TABLE c_employee SET FILEFORMAT ORC; -- Convert to ORC
No rows affected (0.160 seconds)

> ALTER TABLE c_employee CONCATENATE;
```

```
No rows affected (0.165 seconds)
```

 Since v0.8.0, RCFile is added to support fast block-level merging of small RCFiles using the CONCATENATE option. Since v0.14.0, ORC file is added to support the fast stripe-level merging of small ORC files using the CONCATENATE option. Other file formats are not supported yet. RCfiles merge at the block level, while ORC files merge at the stripe level, thereby avoiding the overhead of decompressing and decoding the data.

8. Change the column's data type, position (with AFTER or FIRST), and comment:

```
> DESC employee_internal; -- Check column type before alter
+----------------+----------------------------------+-----------+
|    col_name    |            data_type             |  comment  |
+----------------+----------------------------------+-----------+
| employee_name  | string                           |           |
| work_place     | array<string>                    |           |
| gender_age     | struct<gender:string,age:int>    |           |
| skills_score   | map<string,int>                  |           |
| depart_title   | map<string,array<string>>        |           |
+----------------+----------------------------------+-----------+
5 rows selected (0.119 seconds)

> ALTER TABLE employee_internal
> CHANGE name employee_name string AFTER gender_age;
No rows affected (0.23 seconds)

> DESC employee_internal; -- Verify type and order changes above
+----------------+----------------------------------+-----------+
|    col_name    |            data_type             |  comment  |
+----------------+----------------------------------+-----------+
| work_place     | array<string>                    |           |
| gender_age     | struct<gender:string,age:int>    |           |
| employee_name  | string                           |           |
| skills_score   | map<string,int>                  |           |
| depart_title   | map<string,array<string>>        |           |
+----------------+----------------------------------+-----------+
5 rows selected (0.214 seconds)

> ALTER TABLE employee_internal
> CHANGE employee_name name string COMMENT 'updated' FIRST;
No rows affected (0.238 seconds)
> DESC employee_internal; -- Verify changes by FRIST keywords
+----------------+----------------------------------+-----------+
|    col_name    |            data_type             |  comment  |
+----------------+----------------------------------+-----------+
```

```
| name          | string                                   | updated  |
| work_place    | array<string>                            |          |
| gender_age    | struct<gender:string,age:int>            |          |
| skills_score  | map<string,int>                          |          |
| depart_title  | map<string,array<string>>                |          |
+---------------+------------------------------------------+----------+
5 rows selected (0.119 seconds)
```

9. Add new columns to a table:

```
> ALTER TABLE c_employee ADD COLUMNS (work string);
No rows affected (0.184 seconds)

> DESC c_employee;
+-----------+-------------+-----------+
| col_name  | data_type   | comment   |
+-----------+-------------+-----------+
| name      | string      |           |
| work      | string      |           |
+-----------+-------------+-----------+
2 rows selected (0.115 seconds)
```

10. Replace all columns in a table using the new columns specified:

```
> ALTER TABLE c_employee REPLACE COLUMNS (name string);
No rows affected (0.132 seconds)

> DESC c_employee; -- Verify the changes
+-----------+-------------+-----------+
| col_name  | data_type   | comment   |
+-----------+-------------+-----------+
| name      | string      |           |
+-----------+-------------+-----------+
1 row selected (0.129 seconds)
```

Partitions

By default, a simple HQL query scans the whole table. This slows down the performance when querying a big table. This issue could be resolved by creating partitions, which are very similar to what's in the RDBMS. In Hive, each partition corresponds to a predefined partition column(s), which maps to subdirectories in the table's directory in HDFS. When the table gets queried, only the required partitions (directory) of data in the table are being read, so the I/O and time of the query is greatly reduced. Using partition is a very easy and effective way to improve performance in Hive.

The following is an example of partition creation in HQL:

```
> CREATE TABLE employee_partitioned (
> name STRING,
> work_place ARRAY<STRING>,
> gender_age STRUCT<gender:STRING,age:INT>,
> skills_score MAP<STRING,INT>,
> depart_title MAP<STRING,ARRAY<STRING>>
-- This is regular column
> )
> PARTITIONED BY (year INT, month INT)
-- Use lower case partition column
> ROW FORMAT DELIMITED
> FIELDS TERMINATED BY '|'
> COLLECTION ITEMS TERMINATED BY ','
> MAP KEYS TERMINATED BY ':';
No rows affected (0.293 seconds)

> DESC employee_partitioned;
-- Partition columns are listed twice
```

col_name	data_type	comment
name	string	
work_place	array<string>	
gender_age	struct<gender:string,age:int>	
skills_score	map<string,int>	
depart_title	map<string,array<string>>	
year	int	
month	int	
	NULL	NULL
# Partition Information	NULL	NULL
# col_name	data_type	comment
	NULL	NULL
year	int	
month	int	

```
13 rows selected (0.38 seconds)

> SHOW PARTITIONS employee_partitioned; -- Check partitions
+-------------+
| partition   |
+-------------+
+-------------+
 No rows selected (0.177 seconds)
```

From the preceding result, we can see that the partition is not enabled automatically. We have to use the `ALTER TABLE ADD PARTITION` statement to add static partitions to a table. Here, static means the partition is being added manually. This command changes the table's metadata but does not load data. If the data does not exist in the partition's location, queries will not return any results. To drop the partition metadata, use the `ALTER TABLE ... DROP PARTITION` statement. For external tables, `ALTER` does not change data but metadata, drop partition will not drop data inside the partition. In order to remove data, we can use the `hdfs dfs -rm` command to remove data from HDFS for the external table. For internal tables, `ALTER TABLE ... DROP PARTITION` will remove both partition and data. The following are more examples of common operations on partition tables:

1. Perform partition operations, such as add, remove, and rename partitions:

```
> ALTER TABLE employee_partitioned ADD -- Add multiple static
partitions
> PARTITION (year=2018, month=11) PARTITION (year=2018,
month=12);
No rows affected (0.248 seconds)

> SHOW PARTITIONS employee_partitioned;
+----------------------+
|       partition      |
+----------------------+
| year=2018/month=11   |
| year=2018/month=12   |
+----------------------+
2 rows selected (0.108 seconds)

-- Drop partition with PURGE at the end will remove completely
-- Drop partition will NOT remove data for external table
-- Drop partition will remove data with partition for internal table
> ALTER TABLE employee_partitioned
> DROP IF EXISTS PARTITION (year=2018, month=11);
> SHOW PARTITIONS employee_partitioned;
+----------------------+
|       partition      |
+----------------------+
| year=2018/month=12   |
+----------------------+
1 row selected (0.107 seconds)

> ALTER TABLE employee_partitioned
> DROP IF EXISTS PARTITION (year=2017); -- Drop all partitions in
2017
> ALTER TABLE employee_partitioned
> DROP IF EXISTS PARTITION (month=9); -- Drop all month is 9
```

```
> ALTER TABLE employee_partitioned -- Rename exisiting partition
values
> PARTITION (year=2018, month=12)
> RENAME TO PARTITION (year=2018,month=10);
No rows affected (0.274 seconds)

> SHOW PARTITIONS employee_partitioned;
+---------------------+
| partition           |
+---------------------+
| year=2018/month=10  |
+---------------------+
2 rows selected (0.274 seconds)

-- Below is failed
-- Because all partition columns should be specified for partition
rename
> --ALTER TABLE employee_partitioned PARTITION (year=2018)
> --RENAME TO PARTITION (year=2017);
```

2. Load data into a table partition once the partition is created:

```
> LOAD DATA INPATH '/tmp/hivedemo/data/employee.txt'
> OVERWRITE INTO TABLE employee_partitioned
> PARTITION (year=2018, month=12);
No rows affected (0.96 seconds)

> SELECT name, year, month FROM employee_partitioned; -- Verify data
loaded
+----------+-------+---------+
|   name   | year  | month   |
+----------+-------+---------+
| Michael  | 2018  | 12      |
| Will     | 2018  | 12      |
| Shelley  | 2018  | 12      |
| Lucy     | 2018  | 12      |
+----------+-------+---------+
4 rows selected (37.451 seconds)
```

To avoid manually adding static partitions, dynamic partition insert (or multipartition insert) is designed for dynamically determining which partitions should be added and populated while scanning the input table. This part is introduced in more detail for the INSERT statement in chapter 5, *Data Manipulation*. To populate data in the partition, we can use the LOAD or INSERT statements. The statement only loads the data in the specified partition lists.

Although partition columns map to directory names rather than data, we can query or select them like regular columns in HQL to narrow down the result set.

 The use case for static and dynamic partition is quite different. Static partition is often used for an external table containing data newly landed in HDFS. In this case, it often uses the date, such as `yyyyMMdd`, as the partition column. Whenever the data of the new day arrives, we add the day-specific static partition (by script) to the table, and then the newly arrived data is queryable from the table immediately. For dynamic partition, it is often being used for data transformation between internal tables with partition columns derived from data itself; see `Chapter 5`, *Data Manipulation*.

3. Remove data from the partition. Note, removing data will not remove the partition information. In order to do a complete data cleaning, we can drop the partition described in step 1 after the data is removed:

```
-- For internal table, we use truncate
> TRUNCATE TABLE employee_partitioned PARTITION
(year=2018,month=12);

-- For external table, we have to use hdfs command
> dfs -rm -r -f /user/dayongd/employee_partitioned;
```

4. Add regular columns to a partition table. Note, we CANNOT add new columns as partition columns. There are two options when adding/removing columns from a partition table, CASCADE and RESTRICT. The commonly used CASCADE option cascades the same change to all the partitions in the table. However, RESTRICT is the default, limiting column changes only to table metadata, which means the changes will be only applied to new partitions rather than existing partitions:

```
> ALTER TABLE employee_partitioned ADD COLUMNS (work string)
CASCADE;
```

5. We can change the existing partition column data type:

```
> ALTER TABLE employee_partitioned PARTITION COLUMN(year string);
No rows affected (0.274 seconds)

> DESC employee_partitioned; -- Verify the changes
+---------------------------+---------------------------------+---------+
```

col_name	data_type	comment
name	string	
work_place	array<string>	
gender_age	struct<gender:string,age:int>	
skills_score	map<string,int>	
depart_title	map<string,array<string>>	
work	string	
year	int	
month	int	
	NULL	NULL
# Partition Information	NULL	NULL
# col_name	data_type	comment
	NULL	NULL
year	string	
month	int	

`13 rows selected (0.38 seconds)`

Right now, we can only change the partition column data type. We cannot add/remove a column from partition columns. If we have to change the partition design, we must back up and recreate the table, and then migrate the data. In addition, we are NOT able to change a non-partition table to a partition table directly.

6. Changing the partition's other properties in terms of file format, location, protections, and concatenation have the same syntax to alter the table statement:

```
> ALTER TABLE employee_partitioned PARTITION (year=2018)
> SET FILEFORMAT ORC;
> ALTER TABLE employee_partitioned PARTITION (year=2018)
> SET LOCATION '/tmp/data';
> ALTER TABLE employee_partitioned PARTITION (year=2018) ENABLE
NO_DROP;
> ALTER TABLE employee_partitioned PARTITION (year=2018) ENABLE
OFFLINE;
> ALTER TABLE employee_partitioned PARTITION (year=2018) DISABLE
NO_DROP;
> ALTER TABLE employee_partitioned PARTITION (year=2018) DISABLE
OFFLINE;
> ALTER TABLE employee_partitioned PARTITION (year=2018) CONCATENATE;
```

Buckets

Besides partition, the bucket is another technique to cluster datasets into more manageable parts to optimize query performance. Different from a partition, a bucket corresponds to segments of files in HDFS. For example, the employee_partitioned table from the previous section uses year and month as the top-level partition. If there is a further request to use employee_id as the third level of partition, it creates many partition directories. For instance, we can bucket the employee_partitioned table using employee_id as a bucket column. The value of this column will be hashed by a user-defined number of buckets. The records with the same employee_id will always be stored in the same bucket (segment of files). The bucket columns are defined by CLUSTERED BY keywords. It is quite different from partition columns since partition columns refer to the directory, while bucket columns have to be actual table data columns. By using buckets, an HQL query can easily and efficiently do sampling (see Chapter 6, *Data Aggregation and Sampling*), bucket-side joins, and map-side joins (see Chapter 4, *Data Correlation and Scope*). An example of creating a bucket table is shown as follows:

```
--Prepare table employee_id and its dataset to populate bucket table
> CREATE TABLE employee_id (
> name STRING,
> employee_id INT,
> work_place ARRAY<STRING>,
> gender_age STRUCT<gender:STRING,age:INT>,
> skills_score MAP<STRING,INT>,
> depart_title MAP<STRING,ARRAY<STRING>>
> )
> ROW FORMAT DELIMITED
> FIELDS TERMINATED BY '|'
> COLLECTION ITEMS TERMINATED BY ','
> MAP KEYS TERMINATED BY ':';
No rows affected (0.101 seconds)

> LOAD DATA INPATH
> '/tmp/hivedemo/data/employee_id.txt'
> OVERWRITE INTO TABLE employee_id
No rows affected (0.112 seconds)

--Create the buckets table
> CREATE TABLE employee_id_buckets (
> name STRING,
> employee_id INT,   -- Use this table column as bucket column later
> work_place ARRAY<STRING>,
> gender_age STRUCT<gender:string,age:int>,
> skills_score MAP<string,int>,
```

```
> depart_title MAP<string,ARRAY<string >>
> )
> CLUSTERED BY (employee_id) INTO 2 BUCKETS -- Support more columns
> ROW FORMAT DELIMITED
> FIELDS TERMINATED BY '|'
> COLLECTION ITEMS TERMINATED BY ','
> MAP KEYS TERMINATED BY ':';
No rows affected (0.104 seconds)
```

 To define the proper number of buckets, we should avoid having too much or too little data in each bucket. A better choice is somewhere near two blocks of data, such as 512 MB of data in each bucket. As a best practice, use 2^N as the number of buckets.

Bucketing has a close dependency on the data-loading process. To properly load data into a bucket table, we need to either set the maximum number of reducers to the same number of buckets specified in the table creation (for example, 2), or enable enforce bucketing (recommended), as follows:

```
> set map.reduce.tasks = 2;
No rows affected (0.026 seconds)

> set hive.enforce.bucketing = true; -- This is recommended
No rows affected (0.002 seconds)
```

To populate the data to a bucket table, we cannot use the LOAD DATA statement, because it does not verify the data against the metadata. Instead, INSERT should be used to populate the bucket table all the time:

```
> INSERT OVERWRITE TABLE employee_id_buckets SELECT * FROM employee_id;
No rows affected (75.468 seconds)

-- Verify the buckets in the HDFS from shell
$hdfs dfs -ls /user/hive/warehouse/employee_id_buckets
Found 2 items
-rwxrwxrwx   1 hive hive         900 2018-07-02 10:54
/user/hive/warehouse/employee_id_buckets/000000_0
-rwxrwxrwx   1 hive hive         582 2018-07-02 10:54
/user/hive/warehouse/employee_id_buckets/000001_0
```

Views

Views are logical data structures that can be used to simplify queries by hiding the complexities, such as joins, subqueries, and filters. It is called logical because views are only defined in `metastore` without the footprint in HDFS. Unlike what's in the relational database, views in HQL do not store data or get materialized. Once the view is created, its schema is frozen immediately. Subsequent changes to the underlying tables (for example, adding a column) will not be reflected in the view's schema. If an underlying table is dropped or changed, subsequent attempts to query the invalid view will fail. In addition, views are read-only and may not be used as the target of the `LOAD/INSERT/ALTER` statements.

The following is an example of a view creation statement:

```
> CREATE VIEW IF NOT EXISTS employee_skills
> AS
> SELECT
> name, skills_score['DB'] as DB,
> skills_score['Perl'] as Perl,
> skills_score['Python'] as Python,
> skills_score['Sales'] as Sales,
> skills_score['HR'] as HR
> FROM employee;
No rows affected (0.253 seconds)
```

When creating views, there is no yarn job triggered since this is only a metadata change. However, the job will be triggered when querying the view. To check the view definition, we can use the `SHOW` statement. When modifying the view definition, we can use the `ALTER VIEW` statement. The following are some examples to show, check, and modify the view:

1. Show only views in the database. This was introduced in Hive v2.2.0. We can use the `SHOW TABLES` statement in the earlier version of Hive instead:

   ```
   > SHOW VIEWS;
   > SHOW VIEWS 'employee_*';
   No rows affected (0.19 seconds)
   ```

2. Show the view's definition:

   ```
   > DESC FORMATTED employee_skills;
   > SHOW CREATE TABLE employee_skills; -- this is recommended
   No rows affected (0.19 seconds)
   ```

3. Alter the views' properties:

```
> ALTER VIEW employee_skills SET TBLPROPERTIES ('comment'='A
view');
No rows affected (0.19 seconds)
```

4. Redefine the views:

```
> ALTER VIEW employee_skills as SELECT * from employee;
No rows affected (0.17 seconds)
```

5. Drop the views:

```
> DROP VIEW employee_skills;
No rows affected (0.156 seconds)
```

There is a special view in HQL, called `LateralView`. It is usually used with user-defined table-generating functions in Hive, such as `explode()`, for data normalization or processing JSON data. `LateralView` first applies the table-generation function to the data, and then joins the function's input and output together. See the following examples:

```
> SELECT name, workplace FROM employee_internal

> LATERAL VIEW explode(work_place) wp as workplace;
+----------+------------+
| name     | workplace  |
+----------+------------+
| Michael  | Montreal   |
| Michael  | Toronto    |
| Will     | Montreal   |
| Shelley  | Montreal   |
| Lucy     | Vancouver  |
+----------+------------+
5 rows selected (6.693 seconds)
```

By adding `OUTER` after `LATERAL VIEW`, we can ensure we generate the result even if the table-generating function's output is `NULL`:

```
> SELECT name, workplace FROM employee_internal
> LATERAL VIEW explode(split(null, ',')) wp as workplace;
+-------+------------+
| name  | workplace  |
+-------+------------+
+-------+------------+
No rows selected (5.499 seconds)

> SELECT name, workplace FROM employee_internal
```

```
> LATERAL VIEW OUTER explode(split(null, ',')) wp as workplace;
+---------+-----------+
| name    | workplace |
+---------+-----------+
| Michael | NULL      |
| Michael | NULL      |
| Will    | NULL      |
| Shelley | NULL      |
| Lucy    | NULL      |
+---------+-----------+
5 rows selected (5.745 seconds)
```

Summary

In this chapter, we learned how to define and use various data types in Hive. We looked at how to create, alter, and drop tables, partitions, and views. We also covered how to use external tables, internal tables, partitions, buckets, and views.

In the next chapter, we will dive into the details of querying data in Hive.

Data Correlation and Scope

4

This chapter is about how to discover data by projecting it, linking it, and limiting data ranges or scopes. The chapter mainly covers the syntax and usage of the SELECT, WHERE, LIMIT, JOIN, and UNION/UNION ALL statements to operate on datasets.

In this chapter, we will cover the following topics:

- Projecting data with SELECT
- Filtering data with conditions such as WHERE and LIMIT
- Linking data with JOIN
- Combining data with UNION

Project data with SELECT

The most common use case for Hive is to query data in Hadoop. To achieve this, we need to write and execute a SELECT statement. The typical work done by the SELECT statement is to project the whole row (with SELECT *) or specified columns (with SELECT column1, column2, ...) from a table, with or without conditions.Most simple SELECT statements will not trigger a Yarn job. Instead, a dump task is created just for dumping the data, such as the hdfs dfs -cat command. The SELECT statement is quite often used with the FROM and DISTINCT keywords. A FROM keyword followed by a table is where SELECT projects data. The DISTINCT keyword used after SELECT ensures only unique rows or combination of columns are returned from the table. In addition, SELECT also supports columns combined with user-defined functions, IF(), or a CASE WHEN THEN ELSE END statement, and regular expressions. The following are examples of projecting data with a SELECT statement:

1. Query the whole row or specific columns in the table:

```
> SELECT * FROM employee; -- Project the whole row
```

```
> SELECT name FROM employee; -- Project specified columns
+-----------+
|   name    |
+-----------+
| Michael   |
| Will      |
| Shelley   |
| Lucy      |
+-----------+
4 rows selected (0.452 seconds)

-- List all columns match java regular expression
> SET hive.support.quoted.identifiers = none; -- Enable this
> SELECT `^work.*` FROM employee; -- All columns start with work
+-------------------------+
| employee.work_place     |
+-------------------------+
| ["Montreal","Toronto"]  |
| ["Montreal"]            |
| ["New York"]            |
| ["Vancouver"]           |
+-------------------------+
4 rows selected (0.141 seconds)
```

2. Select distinct columns listed from a table:

```
> SELECT DISTINCT name, work_place FROM employee;
+-----------+------------------------+
| name      | work_place             |
+-----------+------------------------+
| Lucy      | ["Vancouver"]          |
| Michael   | ["Montreal","Toronto"] |
| Shelley   | ["New York"]           |
| Will      | ["Montreal"]           |
+-----------+------------------------+
4 rows selected (35.962 seconds)
```

3. Select columns with IF or CASE WHEN functions:

```
> SELECT
> CASE WHEN gender_age.gender = 'Female' THEN 'Ms.'
> ELSE 'Mr.' END as title,
> name,
> IF(array_contains(work_place, 'New York'), 'US', 'CA') as
country
> FROM employee;
+-------+----------+----------+
| title | name     | country  |
```

```
+-------+---------+---------+
| Mr.   | Michael | CA      |
| Mr.   | Will    | CA      |
| Ms.   | Shelley | US      |
| Ms.   | Lucy    | CA      |
+-------+---------+---------+
4 rows selected (0.585 seconds)
```

Multiple `SELECT` statements can work together to build a complex query using nested queries or CTE. A nested query, which is also called a subquery, is a query projecting data from the result of another query. Nested queries can be rewritten using CTE (mentioned in `Chapter 3`, *Data Definition and Description*) with the `WITH` and `AS` keywords. When using nested queries, an alias should be given for the inner query (see `t1` in the following example), or else Hive will report exceptions. The following are a few examples of using nested queries in HQL:

1. A nested query example with the mandatory alias:

```
> SELECT
> name, gender_age.gender as gender
> FROM (
> SELECT * FROM employee WHERE gender_age.gender = 'Male'
> ) t1; -- t1 here is mandatory
+----------+----------+
|   name   |  gender  |
+----------+----------+
| Michael  | Male     |
| Will     | Male     |
+----------+----------+
2 rows selected (48.198 seconds)
```

2. A nested query can be rewritten with CTE as follows. This is the recommended way of writing a complex single HQL query:

```
> WITH t1 as (
> SELECT * FROM employee WHERE gender_age.gender = 'Male'
> )
> SELECT name, gender_age.gender as gender
> FROM t1;
+----------+----------+
|   name   |  gender  |
+----------+----------+
| Michael  | Male     |
| Will     | Male     |
+----------+----------+
2 rows selected (38.706 seconds)
```

In addition, a special SELECT followed by a constant expression can work without the FROM table clause. It returns the result of the expression. This is equivalent to querying a dummy table with one dummy record:

```
> SELECT concat('1','+','3','=',cast((1 + 3) as string)) as res;
+-------+
| res   |
+-------+
| 1+3=4 |
+-------+
1 row selected (0.109 seconds)
```

Filtering data with conditions

It is quite common to narrow down the result set by using a condition clause, such as LIMIT, WHERE, IN/NOT IN, and EXISTS/NOT EXISTS. The LIMIT keyword limits the specified number of rows returned randomly. Compared with LIMIT, WHERE is a more powerful and generic condition clause to limit the returned result set by expressions, functions, and nested queries as in the following examples:

```
> SELECT name FROM employee LIMIT 2;
+---------+
|  name   |
+---------+
| Lucy    |
| Michael |
+---------+
2 rows selected (71.125 seconds)

> SELECT name, work_place FROM employee WHERE name = 'Michael';
+---------+-----------------------+
| name    | work_place            |
+---------+-----------------------+
| Michael | ["Montreal","Toronto"] |
+---------+-----------------------+
1 row selected (38.107 seconds)

-- All the conditions can use together and use after WHERE
> SELECT name, work_place FROM employee WHERE name = 'Michael' LIMIT 1;
+---------+-----------------------+
| name    | work_place            |
+---------+-----------------------+
| Michael | ["Montreal","Toronto"] |
+---------+-----------------------+
```

```
1 row selected (39.103 seconds)
```

IN/NOT IN is used as an expression to check whether values belong to a set specified by IN or NOT IN. With effect from Hive v2.1.0, IN and NOT IN statements support more than one column:

```
> SELECT name FROM employee WHERE gender_age.age in (27, 30);
+----------+
| name     |
+----------+
| Michael  |
| Shelley  |
+----------+
2 rows selected (0.3 seconds)

-- With multiple columns support after v2.1.0
> SELECT
> name, gender_age
> FROM employee
> WHERE (gender_age.gender, gender_age.age) IN
> (('Female', 27), ('Male', 27 + 3)); -- Also support expression
+----------+------------------------------+
| name     | gender_age                   |
+----------+------------------------------+
| Michael  | {"gender":"Male","age":30}   |
| Shelley  | {"gender":"Female","age":27} |
+----------+------------------------------+
2 rows selected (0.282 seconds)
```

In addition, filtering data can also use a subquery in the WHERE clause with IN/NOT IN and EXISTS/NOT EXISTS. A subquery that uses EXISTS or NOT EXISTS must refer to both inner and outer expressions:

```
> SELECT
> name, gender_age.gender as gender
> FROM employee
> WHERE name IN
> (SELECT name FROM employee WHERE gender_age.gender = 'Male');
+----------+----------+
|   name   |  gender  |
+----------+----------+
| Michael  | Male     |
| Will     | Male     |
+----------+----------+
2 rows selected (54.644 seconds)

> SELECT
```

```
> name, gender_age.gender as gender
> FROM employee a
> WHERE EXISTS (
> SELECT *
> FROM employee b
> WHERE
> a.gender_age.gender = b.gender_age.gender AND
b.gender_age.gender = 'Male'
> ); -- This likes join table a and b with column gender
+-----------+-----------+
|   name    |  gender   |
+-----------+-----------+
| Michael   | Male      |
| Will      | Male      |
+-----------+-----------+
 2 rows selected (69.48 seconds)
```

There are additional restrictions for subqueries used in WHERE clauses:

- Subqueries can only appear on the right-hand side of WHERE clauses
- Nested subqueries are not allowed
- IN/NOT IN in subqueries only support the use of a single column, although they support more in regular expressions

Linking data with JOIN

JOIN is used to link rows from two or more tables together. Hive supports most SQL JOIN operations, such as INNER JOIN and OUTER JOIN. In addition, HQL supports some special joins, such as MapJoin and Semi-Join too. In its earlier version, Hive only supported equal join. After v2.2.0, unequal join is also supported. However, you should be more careful when using unequal join unless you know what is expected, since unequal join is likely to return many rows by producing a Cartesian product of joined tables. When you want to restrict the output of a join, you should apply a WHERE clause after join as JOIN occurs before the WHERE clause. If possible, push filter conditions on the join conditions rather than where conditions to have data filtered earlier. What's more, all types of left/right joins are not commutative and always left/right associative, while INNER and FULL OUTER JOINS are both commutative and associative.

INNER JOIN

`INNER JOIN` or `JOIN` returns rows meeting the join conditions from both sides of joined tables. The `JOIN` keyword can also be omitted by comma-separated table names; this is called an `implicit join`. Here are examples of the HQL JOIN operation:

1. First, prepare a table to join with and load data to it:

```
> CREATE TABLE IF NOT EXISTS employee_hr (
> name string,
> employee_id int,
> sin_number string,
> start_date date
> )
> ROW FORMAT DELIMITED
> FIELDS TERMINATED BY '|';
No rows affected (1.732 seconds)

> LOAD DATA INPATH '/tmp/hivedemo/data/employee_hr.txt'
> OVERWRITE INTO TABLE employee_hr;
No rows affected (0.635 seconds)
```

2. Perform an `INNER JOIN` between two tables with equal and unequal join conditions, along with complex expressions as well as a post join `WHERE` condition. Usually, we need to add a table name or table alias before columns in the join condition, although Hive always tries to resolve them:

```
> SELECT
> emp.name, emph.sin_number
> FROM employee emp
> JOIN employee_hr emph ON emp.name = emph.name; -- Equal Join
+-------------+--------------------+
| emp.name    | emph.sin_number    |
+-------------+--------------------+
| Michael     | 547-968-091        |
| Will        | 527-948-090        |
| Lucy        | 577-928-094        |
+-------------+--------------------+
3 rows selected (71.083 seconds)

> SELECT
> emp.name, emph.sin_number
> FROM employee emp -- Unequal join supported since v2.2.0
returns more rows
```

```
> JOIN employee_hr emph ON emp.name != emph.name;
+----------+------------------+
| emp.name | emph.sin_number  |
+----------+------------------+
| Michael  | 527-948-090      |
| Michael  | 647-968-598      |
| Michael  | 577-928-094      |
| Will     | 547-968-091      |
| Will     | 647-968-598      |
| Will     | 577-928-094      |
| Shelley  | 547-968-091      |
| Shelley  | 527-948-090      |
| Shelley  | 647-968-598      |
| Shelley  | 577-928-094      |
| Lucy     | 547-968-091      |
| Lucy     | 527-948-090      |
| Lucy     | 647-968-598      |
+----------+------------------+
13 rows selected (24.341 seconds)


-- Join with complex expression in join condition
-- This is also the way to implement conditional join
-- Below, conditional ignore row with name = 'Will'
> SELECT
> emp.name, emph.sin_number
> FROM employee emp
> JOIN employee_hr emph ON
> IF(emp.name = 'Will', '1', emp.name) =
> CASE WHEN emph.name = 'Will' THEN '0' ELSE emph.name END;
+----------+------------------+
| emp.name | emph.sin_number  |
+----------+------------------+
| Michael  | 547-968-091      |
| Lucy     | 577-928-094      |
+----------+------------------+
2 rows selected (27.191 seconds)


-- Use where/limit to limit the output of join
> SELECT
> emp.name, emph.sin_number
> FROM employee emp
> JOIN employee_hr emph ON emp.name = emph.name
> WHERE
> emp.name = 'Will';
+----------+------------------+
| emp.name | emph.sin_number  |
+----------+------------------+
| Will     | 527-948-090      |
```

```
+----------+----------------+
1 row selected (26.811 seconds)
```

3. The JOIN operation can be performed on more tables (such as table A, B, and C) with sequence joins. The tables can either join from A to B and B to C, or join from A to B and A to C:

```
> SELECT
> emp.name, empi.employee_id, emph.sin_number
> FROM employee emp
> JOIN employee_hr emph ON emp.name = emph.name
> JOIN employee_id empi ON emp.name = empi.name;
+----------+--------------------+------------------+
| emp.name | empi.employee_id   | emph.sin_number  |
+----------+--------------------+------------------+
| Michael  | 100                | 547-968-091      |
| Will     | 101                | 527-948-090      |
| Lucy     | 103                | 577-928-094      |
+----------+--------------------+------------------+
3 rows selected (67.933 seconds)
```

4. Self-join is where one table joins itself. When doing such joins, a different alias should be given to distinguish the same table:

```
> SELECT
> emp.name -- Use alias before column name
> FROM employee emp
> JOIN employee emp_b -- Here, use a different alias
> ON emp.name = emp_b.name;
+-----------+
| emp.name  |
+-----------+
| Michael   |
| Will      |
| Shelley   |
| Lucy      |
+-----------+
4 rows selected (59.891 seconds)
```

5. Perform an implicit join without using the JOIN keyword. This is only applicable to the INNER JOIN:

```
> SELECT
> emp.name, emph.sin_number
> FROM
> employee emp, employee_hr emph -- Only applies for inner join
> WHERE
```

```
> emp.name = emph.name;
+-------------+-------------------+
| emp.name    | emph.sin_number   |
+-------------+-------------------+
| Michael     | 547-968-091       |
| Will        | 527-948-090       |
| Lucy        | 577-928-094       |
+-------------+-------------------+
3 rows selected (47.241 seconds)
```

6. The join condition uses different columns, which will create an additional job:

```
> SELECT
> emp.name, empi.employee_id, emph.sin_number
> FROM employee emp
> JOIN employee_hr emph ON emp.name = emph.name
> JOIN employee_id empi ON emph.employee_id = empi.employee_id;
+-------------+-------------------+-------------------+
| emp.name    | empi.employee_id  | emph.sin_number   |
+-------------+-------------------+-------------------+
| Michael     | 100               | 547-968-091       |
| Will        | 101               | 527-948-090       |
| Lucy        | 103               | 577-928-094       |
+-------------+-------------------+-------------------+
3 rows selected (49.785 seconds)
```

If `JOIN` uses different columns in its conditions, it will request an additional job to complete the join. If the `JOIN` operation uses the same column in the join conditions, it will join on this condition using one job.

When `JOIN` is performed between multiple tables, Yarn/MapReduce jobs are created to process the data in the HDFS. Each of the jobs is called a stage. Usually, it is suggested to put the big table right at the end of the `JOIN` statement for better performance and to avoid **Out Of Memory (OOM)** exceptions. This is because the last table in the `JOIN` sequence is usually streamed through reducers where as the others are buffered in the reducer by default. Also, a hint, `/*+STREAMTABLE (table_name)*/`, can be specified to advise which table should be streamed over the default decision, as in the following example:

```
> SELECT /*+ STREAMTABLE(employee_hr) */
> emp.name, empi.employee_id, emph.sin_number
> FROM employee emp
> JOIN employee_hr emph ON emp.name = emph.name
> JOIN employee_id empi ON emph.employee_id = empi.employee_id;
```

OUTER JOIN

Besides INNER JOIN, HQL also supports regular OUTER JOIN and FULL JOIN. The logic of such a join is the same as what's in the SQL. The following table summarizes the differences between common joins. Here, we assume table_m has m rows and table_n has n rows with one-to-one mapping:

Join type	Logic	Rows returned
table_m JOIN table_n	This returns all rows matched in both tables.	m ∩ n
table_m LEFT JOIN table_n	This returns all rows in the left table and matched rows in the right table. If there is no match in the right table, it returns NULL in the right table.	m
table_m RIGHT JOIN table_n	This returns all rows in the right table and matched rows in the left table. If there is no match in the left table, it returns NULL in the left table.	n
table_m FULL JOIN table_n	This returns all rows in both tables and matched rows in both tables. If there is no match in the left or right table, it returns NULL instead.	m + n - m ∩ n
table_m CROSS JOIN table_n	This returns all row combinations in both the tables to produce a Cartesian product.	m * n

The following examples demonstrate the different OUTER JOINs:

```
> SELECT
> emp.name, emph.sin_number
> FROM employee emp -- All rows in left table returned
> LEFT JOIN employee_hr emph ON emp.name = emph.name;
+-----------+------------------+
| emp.name  | emph.sin_number  |
+-----------+------------------+
| Michael   | 547-968-091      |
| Will      | 527-948-090      |
| Shelley   | NULL             |   -- NULL for mismatch
| Lucy      | 577-928-094      |
+-----------+------------------+
4 rows selected (39.637 seconds)

> SELECT
> emp.name, emph.sin_number
> FROM employee emp -- All rows in right table returned
> RIGHT JOIN employee_hr emph ON emp.name = emph.name;
```

```
+-----------+-------------------+
| emp.name  | emph.sin_number   |
+-----------+-------------------+
| Michael   | 547-968-091       |
| Will      | 527-948-090       |
| NULL      | 647-968-598       |  -- NULL for mismatch
| Lucy      | 577-928-094       |
+-----------+-------------------+
4 rows selected (34.485 seconds)

> SELECT
> emp.name, emph.sin_number
> FROM employee emp -- Rows from both side returned
> FULL JOIN employee_hr emph ON emp.name = emph.name;
+-----------+-------------------+
| emp.name  | emph.sin_number   |
+-----------+-------------------+
| Lucy      | 577-928-094       |
| Michael   | 547-968-091       |
| Shelley   | NULL              |  -- NULL for mismatch
| NULL      | 647-968-598       |  -- NULL for mismatch
| Will      | 527-948-090       |
+-----------+-------------------+
5 rows selected (64.251 seconds)
```

The CROSS JOIN statement does not have a join condition. The CROSS JOIN statement can also be written using join without condition or with the always true condition, such as 1 = 1. In this case, we can join any datasets with cross joins. However, we only consider using such joins when we have to link data without relations in nature, such as adding headers with a row count to a table. The following are three equal ways of writing CROSS JOIN:

```
> SELECT
> emp.name, emph.sin_number
> FROM employee emp
> CROSS JOIN employee_hr emph;

> SELECT
> emp.name, emph.sin_number
> FROM employee emp
> JOIN employee_hr emph;

> SELECT
> emp.name, emph.sin_number
> FROM employee emp
> JOIN employee_hr emph on 1=1;
+-----------+-------------------+
```

```
| emp.name  | emph.sin_number  |
+-----------+------------------+
| Michael   | 547-968-091      |
| Michael   | 527-948-090      |
| Michael   | 647-968-598      |
| Michael   | 577-928-094      |
| Will      | 547-968-091      |
| Will      | 527-948-090      |
| Will      | 647-968-598      |
| Will      | 577-928-094      |
| Shelley   | 547-968-091      |
| Shelley   | 527-948-090      |
| Shelley   | 647-968-598      |
| Shelley   | 577-928-094      |
| Lucy      | 547-968-091      |
| Lucy      | 527-948-090      |
| Lucy      | 647-968-598      |
| Lucy      | 577-928-094      |
+-----------+------------------+
16 rows selected (34.924 seconds)
```

Although Hive did not support unequal joins explicitly in the earlier version, there are workarounds by using CROSS JOIN and WHERE, as in this example:

```
> SELECT
> emp.name, emph.sin_number
> FROM employee emp
> CROSS JOIN employee_hr emph
> WHERE emp.name <> emph.name;
+-----------+------------------+
| emp.name  | emph.sin_number  |
+-----------+------------------+
| Michael   | 527-948-090      |
| Michael   | 647-968-598      |
| Michael   | 577-928-094      |
| Will      | 547-968-091      |
| Will      | 647-968-598      |
| Will      | 577-928-094      |
| Shelley   | 547-968-091      |
| Shelley   | 527-948-090      |
| Shelley   | 647-968-598      |
| Shelley   | 577-928-094      |
| Lucy      | 547-968-091      |
| Lucy      | 527-948-090      |
| Lucy      | 647-968-598      |
+-----------+------------------+
13 rows selected (35.016 seconds)
```

Special joins

HQL also supports some special joins that we usually do not see in relational databases, such as `MapJoin` and `Semi-join`. `MapJoin` means doing the join operation only with map, without the reduce job. The `MapJoin` statement reads all the data from the small table to memory and broadcasts to all maps. During the map phase, the join operation is performed by comparing each row of data in the big table with small tables against the join conditions. Because there is no reduce needed, such kinds of join usually have better performance. In the newer version of Hive, Hive automatically converts join to `MapJoin` at runtime if possible. However, you can also manually specify the broadcast table by providing a join hint, `/*+ MAPJOIN(table_name) */`. In addition, `MapJoin` can be used for unequal joins to improve performance since both `MapJoin` and `WHERE` are performed in the map phase. The following is an example of using a `MapJoin` hint with `CROSS JOIN`:

```
> SELECT
> /*+ MAPJOIN(employee) */ emp.name, emph.sin_number
> FROM employee emp
> CROSS JOIN employee_hr emph
> WHERE emp.name <> emph.name;
```

The `MapJoin` operation does not support the following:

- Using `MapJoin` after `UNION ALL`, `LATERAL VIEW`, `GROUP BY/JOIN/SORT BY/CLUSTER`, and `BY/DISTRIBUTE BY`
- Using `MapJoin` before `UNION`, `JOIN`, and another `MapJoin`

`Bucket MapJoin` is a special type of `MapJoin` that uses bucket columns (the column specified by `CLUSTERED BY` in the `CREATE TABLE` statement) as the join condition. Instead of fetching the whole table, as done by the `regular MapJoin`, `bucket MapJoin` only fetches the required bucket data. To enable `bucket MapJoin`, we need to enable some settings and make sure the bucket number is are multiple of each other. If both joined tables are sorted and bucketed with the same number of buckets, a sort-merge join can be performed instead of caching all small tables in the memory:

```
> SET hive.optimize.bucketmapjoin = true;
> SET hive.optimize.bucketmapjoin.sortedmerge = true;
> SET hive.input.format =
> org.apache.hadoop.hive.ql.io.BucketizedHiveInputFormat;
```

In addition, the LEFT SEMI JOIN statement is also a type of MapJoin. It is the same as a subquery with IN/EXISTS after v0.13.0 of Hive. However, it is not recommended for use since it is not part of standard SQL:

```
> SELECT a.name FROM employee a
> LEFT SEMI JOIN employee_id b ON a.name = b.name;
```

Combining data with UNION

When we want to combine data with the same schema together, we often use set operations. Regular set operations in the relational database are INTERSECT, MINUS, and UNION/UNION ALL. HQL only supports UNION and UNION ALL. The difference between them is that UNION ALL does not remove duplicate rows while UNION does. In addition, all unioned data must have the same name and data type, or else an implicit conversion will be done and may cause a runtime exception. If ORDER BY, SORT BY, CLUSTER BY, DISTRIBUTE BY, or LIMIT are used, they are applied to the whole result set after the union:

```
> SELECT a.name as nm FROM employee a
> UNION ALL -- Use column alias to make the same name for union
> SELECT b.name as nm FROM employee_hr b;
+-----------+
|    nm     |
+-----------+
| Michael   |
| Will      |
| Shelley   |
| Lucy      |
| Michael   |
| Will      |
| Steven    |
| Lucy      |
+-----------+
8 rows selected (23.919 seconds)

> SELECT a.name as nm FROM employee a
> UNION -- UNION removes duplicated names and slower
> SELECT b.name as nm FROM employee_hr b;
+-----------+
|    nm     |
+-----------+
| Lucy      |
| Michael   |
| Shelley   |
```

```
| Steven   |
| Will     |
+----------+
5 rows selected (32.221 seconds)

-- Order by applies to the unioned data
-- When you want to order only one data set,
-- Use order in the subquery
> SELECT a.name as nm FROM employee a
> UNION ALL
> SELECT b.name as nm FROM employee_hr b
> ORDER BY nm;
+----------+
|    nm    |
+----------+
| Lucy     |
| Lucy     |
| Michael  |
| Michael  |
| Shelley  |
| Steven   |
| Will     |
| Will     |
+----------+
```

For other set operations that HQL does not support yet, such as INTERCEPT and MINUS, we can use joins or left join to implement them as follows:

```
-- Use join for set intercept
> SELECT a.name
> FROM employee a
> JOIN employee_hr b ON a.name = b.name;
+----------+
|  a.name  |
+----------+
| Michael  |
| Will     |
| Lucy     |
+----------+
3 rows selected (44.862 seconds)

-- Use left join for set minus
> SELECT a.name
> FROM employee a
> LEFT JOIN employee_hr b ON a.name = b.name
> WHERE b.name IS NULL;
+----------+
```

```
|   a.name  |
+-----------+
| Shelley   |
+-----------+
1 row selected (36.841 seconds)
```

Summary

In this chapter, you learned to use SELECT statements to project the data needed and filter data with WHERE, LIMIT, IN/EXISTS. Then, we introduced different joins to link datasets together, as well as the dataset operations UNION and UNION ALL. After going through this chapter, you should be able to use the SELECT statement with different WHERE conditions, LIMIT, DISTINCT, and complex subqueries. You should be able to understand and use different types of JOIN statements to link the different datasets horizontally or UNION them vertically.

In the next chapter, we will talk about the details of data exchanging, ordering, and transforming, as well as transactions in HQL.

5
Data Manipulation

The ability to manipulate data is critical in big data analysis. Manipulating data is the process of exchanging, moving, sorting, transforming, and modifying data. This technique is used in many situations, such as cleaning data, searching patterns, creating trends, and so on. HQL offers various statements, keywords, operators, and functions for carrying out data manipulation.

In this chapter, we will cover the following topics:

- Data exchange using `LOAD`, `INSERT`, `IMPORT`, and `EXPORT`
- Data sorting
- Functions
- Transactions and locks

Data exchanging with LOAD

To move data, Hive uses the LOAD statement. *Move* here means the original data is moved to the target table/partition and does not exist in the original place anymore. The LOCAL keyword in the LOAD statement specifies where the files are located on the client host. If the LOCAL keyword is not specified, the files are loaded from the full Uniform Resource Identifier (URI) specified after INPATH (most of the time, hdfs path) or the value from the fs.default.name property defined in hdfs-site.xml by default. The path after INPATH can be a relative path or an absolute path. The path either points to a file or a folder (referring to all files in the folder) to be loaded, but the subfolder is not allowed in the path specified. If the data is loaded into a partition table, the partition column must be specified. The OVERWRITE keyword is used to decide whether to replace the existing data in the target table/partition or not. The following is an example of how to move data to the table or partition from local or HDFS files:

1. Load local data in a table, internal or external. The load statement is not repeatable since the files to be loaded are moved:

```
> LOAD DATA LOCAL INPATH
> '/home/dayongd/Downloads/employee_hr.txt'
> OVERWRITE INTO TABLE employee_hr;
No rows affected (0.436 seconds)
```

2. Load the local data to a partition:

```
> LOAD DATA LOCAL INPATH
> '/home/dayongd/Downloads/employee.txt'
> OVERWRITE INTO TABLE employee_partitioned
> PARTITION (year=2018, month=12);
No rows affected (0.772 seconds)
```

3. Load data from HDFS to a table using the URI:

```
-- Use default fs path
> LOAD DATA INPATH
> '/tmp/hivedemo/data/employee.txt'
> INTO TABLE employee; -- Without OVERWRITE, it appends data
No rows affected (0.453 seconds)

-- Use full URI
> LOAD DATA INPATH
> 'hdfs://localhost:9000/tmp/hivedemo/data/employee.txt'
> OVERWRITE INTO TABLE employee;
No rows affected (0.297 seconds)
```

Data exchange with INSERT

To extract data from tables/partitions, we can use the INSERT keyword. Like other relational databases, Hive supports inserting data into a table by selecting data from another table. This is a very common ETL (a term in data warehousing for Extract, Transform, and Load) pattern used to populate an existing or new table from another table or dataset. The HQL INSERT statement has the same syntax as a relational database's INSERT. However, HQL has improved its INSERT statement by supporting data overwrittening, multi-insert, dynamic partition insert, as well as inserting data into files. The following are a few examples of INSERT statements in HQL:

1. The following is a regular INSERT from the SELECT statement:

```
-- Check the target table, which is empty.
> SELECT name, work_place FROM employee;
+--------------+--------------------+
|employee.name|employee.work_place|
+--------------+--------------------+
+--------------+--------------------+
No rows selected (0.115 seconds)

-- Populate data from query while "INTO" will append data
> INSERT INTO TABLE employee SELECT * FROM ctas_employee;
No rows affected (31.701 seconds)

-- Verify the data loaded
> SELECT name, work_place FROM employee;
+--------------+-----------------------+
|employee.name|  employee.work_place  |
+--------------+-----------------------+
| Michael      |["Montreal","Toronto"]|
| Will         |["Montreal"]           |
| Shelley      |["New York"]           |
| Lucy         |["Vancouver"]          |
+--------------+-----------------------+
4 rows selected (0.12 seconds)
```

2. Insert a table with specified columns. For columns not specified, NULL is populated. However, there are two limitations for now. First, it only works for INSERT INTO rather than INSERT OVERWRITE. Second, unspecified columns must be the primary data type (such as array is not supported). The same limitations also apply to INSERT INTO ... VALUES statements:

```
> CREATE TABLE emp_simple( -- Create a test table only has
primary types
```

```
> name string,
> work_place string
> );
No rows affected (1.479 seconds)

> INSERT INTO TABLE emp_simple (name) -- Specify which columns to
insert
> SELECT name FROM employee WHERE name = 'Will';
No rows affected (30.701 seconds)

> INSERT INTO TABLE emp_simple VALUES -- Insert constant values
> ('Michael', 'Toronto'),('Lucy', 'Montreal');
No rows affected (18.045 seconds)

> SELECT * FROM emp_simple; -- Verify the data loaded
+----------+-------------+
| name     | work_place  |
+----------+-------------+
| Will     | NULL        | -- NULL when column is not specified
| Michael  | Toronto     |
| Lucy     | Montreal    |
+----------+-------------+
3 rows selected (0.263 seconds)
```

3. Insert data from the CTE statement:

```
> WITH a as (
> SELECT * FROM ctas_employee
> )
> FROM a
> INSERT OVERWRITE TABLE employee
> SELECT *;
No rows affected (30.1 seconds)
```

4. Run multi-insert by only scanning the source table once for better performance:

```
> FROM ctas_employee
> INSERT OVERWRITE TABLE employee
> SELECT *
> INSERT OVERWRITE TABLE employee_internal
> SELECT *
> INSERT OVERWRITE TABLE employee_partitioned
> PARTITION (year=2018, month=9) -- Insert to static partition
> SELECT *
> ;
No rows affected (27.919 seconds)
```

The INSERT OVERWRITE statement will replace the data in the target table/partition, while INSERT INTO will append data.

When inserting data into the partitions, we need to specify the partition columns. Instead of specifying static partition values, Hive also supports dynamically giving partition values. Dynamic partitions are useful when it is necessary to populate partitions dynamically from data values. Dynamic partitions are disabled by default because a careless dynamic partition insert could create many partitions unexpectedly. We have to set the following properties to enable dynamic partitions:

```
> SET hive.exec.dynamic.partition=true;
No rows affected (0.002 seconds)
```

By default, the user must specify at least one static partition column. This is to avoid accidentally overwriting partitions. To disable this restriction, we can set the partition mode to nonstrict from the default strict mode before inserting into dynamic partitions as follows:

```
> SET hive.exec.dynamic.partition.mode=nonstrict;
No rows affected (0.002 seconds)

-- Partition year, month are determined from data
> INSERT INTO TABLE employee_partitioned
> PARTITION(year, month)
> SELECT name, array('Toronto') as work_place,
> named_struct("gender","Male","age",30) as gender_age,
> map("Python",90) as skills_score,
> map("R&D",array('Developer')) as depart_title,
> year(start_date) as year, month(start_date) as month
> FROM employee_hr eh
> WHERE eh.employee_id = 102;
No rows affected (29.024 seconds)
```

Complex type constructors are used in the preceding example to create a constant value of a complex data type.

INSERT also supports writing data to files, which is the opposite operation compared to LOAD. It is usually used to extract data from SELECT statements to files in the local/HDFS directory. However, it only supports the OVERWRITE keyword, which means we can only overwrite rather than append data to the data files. By default, the columns are separated by *Ctrl+A* and rows are separated by newlines in the exported file. Column, row, and collection separators can also be overwritten like in the table creation statement. The following are a few examples of exporting data to files using the INSERT OVERWRITE ... directory statement:

1. We can insert to local files with default row separators:

```
> INSERT OVERWRITE LOCAL DIRECTORY '/tmp/output1'
> SELECT * FROM employee;
No rows affected (30.859 seconds)
```

Many partial files could be created by reducers when doing an insert into a directory. To merge them into one file, we can use the HDFS merge command: hdfs dfs -getmerge <exported_hdfs_folder> <local_folder>.

2. Insert into local files with specified row separators:

```
> INSERT OVERWRITE LOCAL DIRECTORY '/tmp/output2'
> ROW FORMAT DELIMITED FIELDS TERMINATED BY ','
> SELECT * FROM employee;
No rows affected (31.937 seconds)

-- Verify the separator
$vi /tmp/output2/000000_0
Michael,Montreal^BToronto,Male^B30,DB^C80,
Product^CDeveloper^DLead
Will,Montreal,Male^B35,Perl^C85,Product^CLead^BTest^CLead
Shelley,New York,Female^B27,Python^C80,Test^CLead^BCOE^CArchitect
Lucy,Vancouver,Female^B57,Sales^C89^BHR^C94,Sales^CLead
```

3. Use multi-insert statements to export data from the same table:

```
> FROM employee
> INSERT OVERWRITE DIRECTORY '/user/dayongd/output3'
> SELECT *
> INSERT OVERWRITE DIRECTORY '/user/dayongd/output4'
> SELECT name ;
No rows affected (25.4 seconds)
```

Combined HQL and HDFS shell commands, we can extract data to local or remote files with both append and overwrite supported. The `hive -e quoted_hql_string` or `hive -f <hql_filename>` commands can execute a HQL query or query file. Linux's redirect operators and piping can be used with these commands to redirect result sets. The following are a few examples:

- **Append to local files**: `$hive -e 'select * from employee' >> test`
- **Overwrite local files**: `$hive -e 'select * from employee' > test`
- **Append to HDFS files**: `$hive -e 'select * from employee'|hdfs dfs -appendToFile - /tmp/test1`
- **Overwrite HDFS files**: `$hive -e 'select * from employee'|hdfs dfs -put -f - /tmp/test2`

Data exchange with [EX|IM]PORT

When working on data migration or release deployment, we may need to move data between different environments or clusters. In HQL, `EXPORT` and `IMPORT` statements are available to move data between HDFS in different environments or clusters. The `EXPORT` statement exports both data and metadata from a table or partition. Metadata is exported in a file called `_metadata`. Data is exported in a subdirectory called data, as follows:

```
> EXPORT TABLE employee TO '/tmp/output5';
No rows affected (0.19 seconds)
> dfs -ls -R /tmp/output5/;
+--------------------------------+
|            DFS Output          |
+--------------------------------+
| ... /tmp/output5/_metadata     |
| ... /tmp/output5/data          |
| ... /tmp/output5/data/000000_0 |
+--------------------------------+
3 rows selected (0.014 seconds)
```

For `EXPORT`, the database name can be used before the table name without any syntax error, but the database is useless and ignored by the `IMPORT` statement.

Once exported, we can copy exported files to other clusters manually or with the `hadoop distcp <srcurl> <desturl>` command. Then, we can import data in the following ways:

1. Import data into a new table. If the table exists, it will throw an error:

```
> IMPORT TABLE FROM '/tmp/output5'; -- By default, use exported
name
Error: Error while compiling statement: FAILED: SemanticException
[Error 10119]: Table exists and contains data files
(state=42000, code=10119)
> IMPORT TABLE empolyee_imported -- Specify a table imported
> FROM '/tmp/output5';
No rows affected (0.788 seconds)
```

2. Import data to an external table, where the `LOCATION` property is optional:

```
> IMPORT EXTERNAL TABLE empolyee_imported_external
> FROM '/tmp/output5'
> LOCATION '/tmp/output6';
No rows affected (0.256 seconds)
```

3. Export and import partitions:

```
> EXPORT TABLE employee_partitioned partition
> (year=2018, month=12) TO '/tmp/output7';
No rows affected (0.247 seconds)
> IMPORT TABLE employee_partitioned_imported
> FROM '/tmp/output7';
No rows affected (0.14 seconds)
```

Data sorting

Another aspect of manipulating data is properly sorting it in order to clearly identify important facts, such as top the N values, maximum, minimum, and so on. HQL supports the following keywords for data sorting:

1. ORDER BY [ASC|DESC]: It is similar to the SQL ORDER BY statement. When using ORDER BY, a sorted order is maintained across all of the output from every reducer. It performs a global sort using only one reducer, so it takes longer to return the result. The direction specifier after ORDER BY can be either ASC for ascending (low to high) or DESC for descending (high to low). If you do not provide a direction specifier, the default of ascending is used. Since v2.1.0, the ORDER BY statement supports specifying the sorting direction for the NULL value, such as NULL FIRST or NULL LAST. By default, NULL stays at the first place in the ASC direction and the last place in the DESC direction:

```
> SELECT name FROM employee ORDER BY name DESC; -- By columns
+----------+
|   name   |
+----------+
| Will     |
| Shelley  |
| Michael  |
| Lucy     |
+----------+
4 rows selected (24.057 seconds)

> SELECT name
> FROM employee   -- Order by expression
> ORDER BY CASE WHEN name = 'Will' THEN 0 ELSE 1 END DESC;
+----------+
|   name   |
+----------+
| Lucy     |
| Shelley  |
| Michael  |
| Will     |
+----------+
4 rows selected (25.057 seconds)

> SELECT * FROM emp_simple ORDER BY work_place NULL LAST;
+----------+-------------+
| name     | work_place  |
+----------+-------------+
| Lucy     | Montreal    |
| Michael  | Toronto     |
| Will     | NULL        |   -- NULL stays at the last
+----------+-------------+
3 rows selected (0.263 seconds)
```

Using LIMIT with ORDER BY is strongly recommended. When the
hive.mapred.mode = strict property is set (the default value
for hive.mapred.mode is nonstrict in Hive v1.* and strict in Hive
v2.*), it throws exceptions when using ORDER BY without LIMIT.

2. SORT BY [ASC|DESC]: It specifies which columns to use to sort reducer input
records. This means the sorting is completed before sending data to the reducer.
The SORT BY statement does not perform a global sort (but ORDER BY does) and
only ensures data is locally sorted in each reducer. If SORT BY sorts with
only one reducer (set mapred.reduce.tasks=1), it is equal to ORDER BY, as
the following example shows. Most of the time, SORT BY itself is useless but is
used with DISTRIBUTE BY, which is introduced next:

```
> SET mapred.reduce.tasks = 2; -- Sort by with more than 1 reducer
No rows affected (0.001 seconds)

> SELECT name FROM employee SORT BY name DESC;
+----------+
|   name   |
+----------+
| Shelley  | -- Once result is collected to client, it is
| Michael  |    order-less
| Lucy     |
| Will     |
+----------+
4 rows selected (54.386 seconds)
> SET mapred.reduce.tasks = 1; -- Sort by one reducer
No rows affected (0.002 seconds)

> SELECT name FROM employee SORT BY name DESC;
+-----------+
|   name    |
+-----------+
| Will      | -- Same result to ORDER BY
| Shelley   |
| Michael   |
| Lucy      |
+-----------+
4 rows selected (46.03 seconds)
```

3. DISTRIBUTE BY: It is very similar to GROUP BY (introduced in `Chapter 6, Data Aggregation and Sampling`) when the mapper decides to which reducer it can deliver the output. Compared to GROUP BY, DISTRIBUTE BY will not work on data aggregations, such as count(*), but only directs where data goes. In this case, DISTRIBUTE BY is quite often used to reorganize data in files by specified columns. For example, we may need to use DISTRIBUTE BY after a UNION result set to reorganize data in higher granularity. When used with SORT BY to sort data within specified groups, DISTRIBUTE BY can be used before SORT BY in one query. In addition, the columns after DISTRIBUTE BY must appear in the select column list as follows:

```
-- Error when not specify distributed column employee_id in
select
> SELECT name FROM employee_hr DISTRIBUTE BY employee_id;
Error: Error while compiling statement: FAILED: SemanticException
[Error 10004]: Line 1:44 Invalid table alias or column reference
'employee_id': (possible column names are: name)

> SELECT name, employee_id FROM employee_hr DISTRIBUTE BY
employee_id;
+-----------+---------------+
|   name    |  employee_id  |
+-----------+---------------+
| Lucy      | 103           |
| Steven    | 102           |
| Will      | 101           |
| Michael   | 100           |
+-----------+---------------+
4 rows selected (38.92 seconds)

-- Used with SORT BY to order name started on the same day
> SELECT name, start_date
> FROM employee_hr
> DISTRIBUTE BY start_date SORT BY name;
+-----------+---------------+
|   name    |  start_date   |
+-----------+---------------+
| Lucy      | 2010-01-03    |
| Michael   | 2014-01-29    |
| Steven    | 2012-11-03    |
| Will      | 2013-10-02    |
+-----------+---------------+
4 rows selected (38.01 seconds)
```

4. CLUSTER BY: It is a shortcut operator you can use to perform DISTRIBUTE BY and SORT BY operations on the same group of columns. The CLUSTER BY statement does not allow you to specify ASC or DESC yet. Compared to ORDER BY, which is globally sorted, the CLUSTER BY statement sorts data in each distributed group:

```
> SELECT name, employee_id FROM employee_hr CLUSTER BY name;
+-----------+---------------+
|   name    |  employee_id  |
+-----------+---------------+
| Lucy      | 103           |
| Michael   | 100           |
| Steven    | 102           |
| Will      | 101           |
+-----------+---------------+
4 rows selected (39.791 seconds)
```

When we have to do a global sort, we can do CLUSTER BY first and then ORDER BY. In this way, we can fully utilize all the available reducers ahead of ORDER BY and have better performance, for example: SELECT * FROM (SELECT * FROM employee CLUSTER BY name) base ORDER BY name;.

In summary, the difference between these sorting keywords is shown in the following diagram:

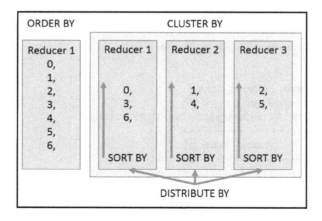

HQL sorting keywords difference

Functions

To further manipulate data, we can also use operators, expressions, and functions in HQL to transform data. The Hive wiki (`https://cwiki.apache.org/confluence/display/Hive/LanguageManual+UDF`) offers specifications for all supported expressions and functions, so we do not want to repeat all of them here, except a few important tips in this chapter.

Hive has defined relational operators, arithmetic operators, logical operators, complex type operators, and complex type constructors. For relational, arithmetic, and logical operators, they are similar to standard operators in SQL/Java. For operators on a complex data type, we have already introduced them in the *Understanding Hive data types* Section in `Chapter 3`, *Data Definition and Description*, as well as the example of inserting data into dynamic partitions earlier in this chapter. Functions in HQL are categorized as follows:

- **Mathematical functions**: They are mainly used to perform mathematical calculations, such as `rand(...)` and `pi(...)`
- **Collection functions**: They are used to find the size, keys, and values for complex types, such as `size(...)`
- **Type conversion functions**: These are mainly `cast(...)` and `binary(...)` functions to convert one type to another
- **Date functions**: They are used to perform date-related calculations, such as `year(...)` and `month(...)`
- **Conditional functions**: They are used to check specific conditions with a defined value returned, such as `coalesce(...)`, `if(...)`, and case when then `else` end
- **String functions**: They are used to perform string-related operations, such as `upper(...)` and `trim(...)`
- **Aggregate functions**: They are used to perform aggregation (introduced in the next chapter), such as `sum(...)` and `count(*)`
- **Table-generating functions**: These functions transform a single input row into multiple output rows, such as `explode(...)` and `json_tuple(...)`
- **Customized functions**: These functions are created by Java as extensions, and are introduced in `Chapter 8`, *Extensibility Considerations*

To list all operators, built-in functions, and user-defined functions, we can use the SHOW FUNCTIONS commands. For more details of a specific function, we can use DESC [EXTENDED] function_name as follows:

```
> SHOW FUNCTIONS; -- List all functions
> DESCRIBE FUNCTION <function_name>; -- Detail for the function
> DESCRIBE FUNCTION EXTENDED <function_name>; -- More details
```

The following are some tips and best practices using HQL functions with examples.

Function tips for collections

The size(...) function is used to calculate the collection size for the MAP, ARRAY, or nested MAP/ARRAY. It returns −1 if the collection is NULL and returns 0 if the collection is empty, as follows:

```
> SELECT
> SIZE(work_place) as array_size,
> SIZE(skills_score) as map_size,
> SIZE(depart_title) as complex_size,
> SIZE(depart_title["Product"]) as nest_size
> FROM employee;
+-------------+-----------+---------------+------------+
| array_size  | map_size  | complex_size  | nest_size  |
+-------------+-----------+---------------+------------+
| 2           | 1         | 1             | 2          |
| 1           | 1         | 2             | 1          |
| 1           | 1         | 2             | -1         |
| 1           | 2         | 1             | -1         |
+-------------+-----------+---------------+------------+
4 rows selected (0.062 seconds)

> SELECT size(null), size(array(null)), size(array());
+-----+-----+-----+
| _c0 | _c1 | _c2 |
+-----+-----+-----+
| -1  | 1   | 0   |
+-----+-----+-----+
1 row selected (11.453 seconds)
```

The array_contains(...) function checks whether an array contains some values or not and returns TRUE or FALSE. The sort_array(...) function sorts the array in ascending order. These can be used as follows:

```
> SELECT
> array_contains(work_place, 'Toronto') as is_Toronto,
> sort_array(work_place) as sorted_array
> FROM employee;
+--------------+----------------------------+
| is_toronto   |        sorted_array        |
+--------------+----------------------------+
| true         | ["Montreal","Toronto"]     |
| false        | ["Montreal"]               |
| false        | ["New York"]               |
| false        | ["Vancouver"]              |
+--------------+----------------------------+
4 rows selected (0.059 seconds)
```

Function tips for date and string

The `to_date(...)` function removes hours, minutes, and seconds from a date. This is useful when we need to check whether the values of date/time type columns are within the data range, such as `to_date(update_datetime)` between 2014-11-01 and 2014-11-31. `to_date(...)` can be used as follows:

```
> SELECT TO_DATE(FROM_UNIXTIME(UNIX_TIMESTAMP())) as currentdate;
+-----------------+
| currentdate     |
+-----------------+
| 2018-05-15      |
+-----------------+
1 row selected (0.153 seconds)
```

The `reverse(...)` function reverses the order of each letter in a string. The `split(...)` function tokenizes the string using a specified tokenizer. Here is an example of using both of them to get the filename from a path:

```
> SELECT
> reverse(split(reverse('/home/user/employee.txt'),'/')[0])
> as linux_file_name;
+-------------------+
| linux_file_name   |
+-------------------+
| employee.txt      |
+-------------------+
1 row selected (0.1 seconds)
```

Whereas `explode(...)` outputs each element in an array or map as separate rows, `collect_set(...)` and `collect_list(...)` do the opposite by returning a set/list of elements from each group. The `collect_set(...)` statement will remove duplications from the result, but `collect_list(...)` does not:

```
> SELECT
> collect_set(gender_age.gender) as gender_set,
> collect_list(gender_age.gender) as gender_list
> FROM employee;
+-------------------+-----------------------------------+
| gender_set        | gender_list                       |
+-------------------+-----------------------------------+
| ["Male","Female"] | ["Male","Male","Female","Female"] |
+-------------------+-----------------------------------+
1 row selected (24.488 seconds)
```

Virtual column functions

Virtual columns are special functions in HQL. Right now, there are two virtual columns: `INPUT__FILE__NAME` and `BLOCK__OFFSET__INSIDE__FILE`. The `INPUT__FILE__NAME` function shows the input file's name for a mapper task. The `BLOCK__OFFSET__INSIDE__FILE` function shows the current global file position or the current block's file offset if the file is compressed. The following are examples of using virtual columns to find out where data is physically located in HDFS, especially for bucketed and partitioned tables:

```
> SELECT
> INPUT__FILE__NAME,BLOCK__OFFSET__INSIDE__FILE as OFFSIDE
> FROM employee;
+------------------------------------------------------------------+---------+
| input__file__name                                                | offside |
+------------------------------------------------------------------+---------+
| hdfs://localhost:9000/user/hive/warehouse/employee/000000_0 | 0       |
| hdfs://localhost:9000/user/hive/warehouse/employee/000000_0 | 62      |
| hdfs://localhost:9000/user/hive/warehouse/employee/000000_0 | 115     |
| hdfs://localhost:9000/user/hive/warehouse/employee/000000_0 | 176     |
+------------------------------------------------------------------+---------+
4 rows selected (0.47 seconds)
```

Transactions and locks

ACID (Atomicity, Consistency, Isolation, and Durability) is a long-expected Hive feature, and builds a foundation for relational databases; it has been available since Hive v0.14.0. Full ACID support in Hive is implemented through row-level transactions and locks. This makes it possible for Hive to deal with use cases such as concurrent read/write, data cleaning, data modification, complex ETL/SCD (Slow Changing Dimensions), streaming data ingest, bulk data merge, and so on. In this section, we'll introduce them in more detail.

Transactions

For now, all transactions in HQL are auto-committed without supporting `BEGIN`, `COMMIT`, and `ROLLBACK`, like as with relational databases. Also, the table that has a transaction feature enabled has to be a bucket table with the `ORC` file format. The following configuration parameters must be set appropriately in `hive-site.xml` or beeline connection string to turn on transaction support:

```
> SET hive.support.concurrency = true;
> SET hive.enforce.bucketing = true;
> SET hive.exec.dynamic.partition.mode = nonstrict;
> SET hive.txn.manager =
> org.apache.hadoop.hive.ql.lockmgr.DbTxnManager;
> SET hive.compactor.initiator.on = true;
> SET hive.compactor.worker.threads = 1;
```

When a transaction is enabled, each transaction-related operation, such as `INSERT`, `UPDATE`, and `DELETE`, stores data in delta files. At read time, the reader merges the base and delta files, applying any updates and deletes. Both base and delta directory names contain the transaction IDs. Occasionally, these changes need to be merged into the base files by compactors, which are background processes in the `metastore`, for better performance and smaller file size. To see a list of all tables/partitions currently being compacted or scheduled for compaction, use the `SHOW COMPACTIONS` statement.

Then, create a table with transactions enabled in the table properties and populate the data:

```
> CREATE TABLE employee_trans (
> emp_id int,
> name string,
> start_date date,
> quit_date date,
> quit_flag string
> )
> CLUSTERED BY (emp_id) INTO 2 BUCKETS STORED as ORC
> TBLPROPERTIES ('transactional'='true'); -- Also need to set this
No rows affected (2.216 seconds)

> INSERT INTO TABLE employee_trans VALUES
> (100, 'Michael', '2017-02-01', null, 'N'),
> (101, 'Will', '2017-03-01', null, 'N'),
> (102, 'Steven', '2018-01-01', null, 'N'),
> (104, 'Lucy', '2017-10-01', null, 'N');
No rows affected (48.216 seconds)
```

For a table with transactions enabled, we can perform UPDATE, DELETE, and MERGE operations on data.

UPDATE statement

The UPDATE statement is used to update one or more columns in a table when certain conditions are met. Here, the updated columns cannot partition columns or bucket columns. The value used for updating should be an expression or constant rather than a subquery:

```
> UPDATE employee_trans
> SET quite_date = current_date, quit_flag = 'Y'
> WHERE emp_id = 104;
No rows affected (39.745 seconds)

> SELECT
> quit_date, quit_flag
> FROM employee_trans
> WHERE emp_id = 104; -- Verify the update
+-------------+------------+
| quit_date   | quit_flag  |
+-------------+------------+
| 2018-04-20  | Y          |
+-------------+------------+
1 row selected (0.325 seconds)
```

DELETE statement

The DELETE statement is used to remove one or more rows from a table when a certain condition is met as follows:

```
> DELETE FROM employee_trans WHERE emp_id = 104;
No rows affected (42.298 seconds)

-- Verify the result, deleted
> SELECT name FROM employee_trans WHERE emp_id = 104;
+------+
| name |
+------+
+------+
No rows selected (0.33 seconds)
```

MERGE statement

The MERGE statement, available since Hive 2.2, is used to perform UPDATE, DELETE, or INSERT on a target table, based on the JOIN condition matching or not against a source table or query. The standard syntax is as follows:

```
MERGE INTO <target_table> as Target USING <source_query/table> as Source
ON <join_condition between two tables>
WHEN MATCHED [AND <boolean expression>] THEN UPDATE SET <set clause list>
WHEN MATCHED [AND <boolean expression>] THEN DELETE
WHEN NOT MATCHED [AND <boolean expression>] THEN INSERT VALUES <value list>
```

The current limitations for the MERGE INTO statement are as follows:

- One, two, or three WHEN clauses may be present
- At most one of each type of UPDATE/DELETE/INSERT can be used
- WHEN NOT MATCHED must be the last clause and only supports INSERT VALUES <value_list>
- WHEN MATCHED only supports UPDATE or DELETE
- If both UPDATE and DELETE clauses are present, the first one in the statement must include [AND <boolean expression>]

Here is an example of merging data in HQL:

```
-- Create another table as merge source
> CREATE TABLE employee_update (
> emp_id int,
> name string,
> start_date date,
> quit_date date,
> quit_flag string
> );
No rows affected (0.127 seconds)

-- Populate data
> INSERT INTO TABLE employee_update VALUES
> (100, 'Michael', '2017-02-01', '2018-01-01', 'Y'), -- People quit
> (102, 'Steven', '2018-01-02', null, 'N'), -- People has start_date update
> (105, 'Lily', '2018-04-01', null, 'N'); -- People newly started
No rows affected (19.832 seconds)

-- Do a data merge from employee_update to employee_trans
> MERGE INTO employee_trans as tar USING employee_update as src
> ON tar.emp_id = src.emp_id
> WHEN MATCHED and src.quit_flag <> 'Y' THEN UPDATE SET start_date
src.start_date
> WHEN MATCHED and src.quit_flag = 'Y' THEN DELETE
> WHEN NOT MATCHED THEN INSERT VALUES (src.emp_id, src.name,
src.start_date, src.quit_date, src.quit_flag);
No rows affected (174.357 seconds)

SELECT * FROM employee_trans; -- Verify the result, Michael is deleted
+---------+---------+-------------+------------+------------+
| emp_id  | name    |start_date   | quit_date  | quit_flag  |
+---------+---------+-------------+------------+------------+
| 102     | Steven  | 2018-01-02  | NULL       | N          | -- Update
| 101     | Will    | 2017-03-01  | NULL       | N          |
| 105     | Lily    | 2018-04-01  | NULL       | N          | -- Insert
+---------+---------+-------------+------------+------------+
3 rows selected (0.356 seconds)
```

In HQL, the SHOW TRANSACTIONS statement is available to show currently open and aborted transactions in the system. When we run the previous queries, we can open another Hive connection and issue this statement to see the current transactions:

```
> SHOW TRANSACTIONS;
+-----+-----+--------------+------------------+--------+----------+
|txnid|state|startedtime   |lastheartbeattime|user    |host      |
+-----+-----+--------------+------------------+--------+----------+
|2    |OPEN |1524183790000|1524183790000     |vagrant |vagrant.vm|
+-----+-----+--------------+------------------+--------+----------+
2 rows selected (0.063 seconds)
```

The ABORT TRANSACTIONS transaction_id statement has been used to kill a transaction with a specified ID since Hive v2.1.0.

Locks

Locks ensure data isolation as described in the ACID principle. Hive has supported concurrency access and locking mechanisms since v0.7.0 and updated to a new lock manager in v0.13.0. There are two types of lock provided as follows:

- **Shared lock:** Also called s lock, it allows being shared concurrently. This is acquired when a table/partition is read.
- **Exclusive lock**: Also called x lock. This is acquired for all other operations that modify the table/partition.

For partition tables, only a shared lock is acquired if the change is only applicable to the newly-created partitions. An exclusive lock is acquired on the table if the change is applicable to all partitions. In addition, an exclusive lock on the table globally affects all partitions. For more information regarding locks, see https://cwiki.apache.org/confluence/display/Hive/Locking.

To enable locking, make sure the two properties are set in a Hive session or hive-site.xml (refer *Transaction*, section above):

- hive.support.concurrency = true
- hive.txn.manager = org.apache.hadoop.hive.ql.lockmgr.DbTxnManager

Any query must acquire proper locks before being allowed to perform corresponding lock-permitted operations. When the query is SELECT, it will get an S lock. Concurrent SELECT statements on the same table will get multiple S locks and run in parallel. When the query is INSERT, it will get an X lock. Concurrent INSERT statements will only get one X lock, so an INSERT has to wait until the lock is released by the other INSERT. In addition, a table can only have one X lock. When trying to get an X lock, there should no other locks on the table, or else the operation that requires an X lock, such as INSERT, ALTER, has to wait and retry (the hive.lock.sleep.between.retries property controls the retry time).

By using the new lock manager, DbTxnManager, locks can only be acquired/released from a query implicitly. To see the locks on the table, use the SHOW LOCKS/SHOW LOCKS table_name statement:

```
-- Show all locks when running merge into above
> SHOW LOCKS;
+---------+----------+-----------------+-------------+-------------+
| lockid  | database | table           | lock_state  | lock_type   |
+---------+----------+-----------------+-------------+-------------+
| 19.1    | default  | employee_update | ACQUIRED    | SHARED_READ |
| 19.2    | default  | employee_trans  | ACQUIRED    |SHARED_WRITE |
+---------+----------+-----------------+-------------+-------------+
3 rows selected (0.059 seconds)
```

Summary

In this chapter, we covered how to exchange data between tables and files using the LOAD, INSERT, IMPORT, and EXPORT keywords. Then, we introduced the different data ordering and sorting options. We also covered some commonly used tips on using functions. Finally, we provided an overview of row-level transactions, DELETE, UPDATE, MERGE, and locks. After going through this chapter, we should be able to import or export data with HQL. We should be experienced in using different types of data sorting keywords, functions, and transaction statements.

In the next chapter, we'll look at the different ways of carrying out data aggregations and sampling in HQL.

Data Aggregation and Sampling

6

This chapter is about how to aggregate and sample data in HQL. It first covers the use of several aggregate functions, enhanced aggregate functions, and window functions working with a GROUP BY, PARTITION BY statement. Then, it introduces the different ways of sampling data. In this chapter, we will cover the following topics:

- Basic aggregation
- Enhanced aggregation
- Aggregation condition
- Window functions
- Sampling

Basic aggregation

Data aggregation is the process of gathering and expressing data in a summary to get more information about particular groups based on specific conditions. HQL offers several built-in aggregate functions, such as max(...), min(...), and avg(...). It also supports advanced aggregation using keywords such as GROUPING SETS, ROLLUP, and CUBE, and different types of window function.

The basic built-in aggregate functions are usually used with the GROUP BY clause. If there is no GROUP BY clause specified, it aggregates over the whole row (all columns) by default. Besides aggregate functions, all columns selected must also be included in the GROUP BY clause. The following are a few examples involving the built-in aggregate functions:

1. Aggregation without GROUP BY columns:

```
> SELECT
> count(*) as rowcnt1,
> count(1) as rowcnt2 -- same to count(*)
> FROM employee;
```

```
+---------+---------+
| rowcnt1 | rowcnt2 |
+---------+---------+
| 4       | 4       |
+---------+---------+
1 row selected (0.184 seconds)
```

Sometimes, the basic aggregate function call returns the result immediately, such as in the previous example, where it took less than 0.2 seconds. The reason is that Hive fetches such aggregation results directly from the statistics collected (introduced in Chapter 8, *Extensibility Considerations*). To get the aggregation by actually running a job, you may need to add a limit or where clause in the query.

2. Aggregation with GROUP BY columns:

```
> SELECT
> gender_age.gender, count(*) as row_cnt
> FROM employee
> GROUP BY gender_age.gender;
+--------------------+---------+
| gender_age.gender  | row_cnt |
+--------------------+---------+
| Female             | 2       |
| Male               | 3       |
+--------------------+---------+
2 rows selected (100.565 seconds)

-- The column name selected is not a group by columns causes error
> SELECT
> name, gender_age.gender, count(*) as row_cnt
> FROM employee GROUP BY gender_age.gender;
Error: Error while compiling statement: FAILED: SemanticException
[Error 10025]: Line 2:1 Expression
not in GROUP BY key 'name' (state=42000,code=10025)
```

If we have to select columns that are not GROUP BY columns, one way is to use window functions, which are introduced later.

An aggregate function can be used with other aggregate functions in the same SELECT statement. It can also be used with other functions, such as conditional functions, in a nested way. However, nested aggregate functions are not supported. See the following examples for more details:

1. Multiple aggregate functions in the same SELECT statement:

```
> SELECT
> gender_age.gender, avg(gender_age.age) as avg_age,
> count(*) as row_cnt
> FROM employee GROUP BY gender_age.gender;
+--------------------+----------------------+----------+
| gender_age.gender  |       avg_age        | row_cnt  |
+--------------------+----------------------+----------+
| Female             | 42.0                 | 2        |
| Male               | 31.666666666666668   | 3        |
+--------------------+----------------------+----------+
2 rows selected (98.857 seconds)
```

2. Aggregate functions can also be used with CASE WHEN THEN ELSE END, coalesce(...), or if(...):

```
> SELECT
> sum(CASE WHEN gender_age.gender = 'Male'
> THEN gender_age.age ELSE 0 END)/
> count(CASE WHEN gender_age.gender = 'Male' THEN 1
> ELSE NULL END) as male_age_avg
> FROM employee;
+----------------------+
|     male_age_avg     |
+----------------------+
| 31.666666666666668   |
+----------------------+
1 row selected (38.415 seconds)

> SELECT
> sum(coalesce(gender_age.age,0)) as age_sum,
> sum(if(gender_age.gender = 'Female',gender_age.age,0)) as
female_age_sum
> FROM employee;
+----------+----------------+
| age_sum  | female_age_sum |
+----------+----------------+
| 179      | 84             |
+----------+----------------+
1 row selected (42.137 seconds)
```

3. GROUP BY can also apply to expressions:

```
> SELECT
> if(name = 'Will', 1, 0) as name_group,
> count(name) as name_cnt
> FROM employee
> GROUP BY if(name = 'Will', 1, 0);
+-------------+-----------+
| name_group | name_cnt |
+-------------+-----------+
| 0          | 3         |
| 1          | 1         |
+-------------+-----------+
2 rows selected (23.749 seconds)
```

4. Verify that nested aggregate functions are not allowed:

```
> SELECT avg(count(*)) as row_cnt FROM employee;
Error: Error while compiling statement: FAILED: SemanticException
[Error 10128]: Line 1:11 Not yet
supported place for UDAF 'count' (state=42000,code=10128)
```

5. Aggregate functions such as max(...) or min(...) apply to NULL and return NULL. However, functions such as sum() and avg(...) cannot apply to NULL. The count(null) returns 0.

```
> SELECT max(null), min(null), count(null);
+------+------+-----+
| _c0 | _c1 | _c2 |
+------+------+-----+
| NULL | NULL | 0 |
+------+------+-----+
1 row selected (23.54 seconds)

> SELECT sum(null), avg(null);
Error: Error while compiling statement: FAILED:
UDFArgumentTypeException Only numeric or string type
arguments are accepted but void is passed.
(state=42000,code=40000)
```

In addition, we may encounter a very special behavior when dealing with aggregation across columns with a NULL value. The entire row (if one column has NULL as a value in the row) will be ignored. To avoid this, we can use coalesce(...) to assign a default value when the column value is NULL. See the following example:

```
-- Create a table t for testing
> CREATE TABLE t (val1 int, val2 int);
> INSERT INTO TABLE t VALUES (1, 2),(null,2),(2,3);
No rows affected (0.138 seconds)

-- Check the rows in the table created
> SELECT * FROM t;
+---------+---------+
| t.val1  | t.val2  |
+---------+---------+
| 1       | 2       |
| NULL    | 2       |
| 2       | 3       |
+---------+---------+
3 rows selected (0.069 seconds)

-- The 2nd row (NULL, 2) is ignored when doing sum(val1 + val2)
> SELECT sum(val1), sum(val1 + val2) FROM t;
+------+------+
| _c0  | _c1  |
+------+------+
| 3    | 8    |
+------+------+
1 row selected (57.775 seconds)

> SELECT
> sum(coalesce(val1,0)),
> sum(coalesce(val1,0) + val2)
> FROM t;
+------+------+
| _c0  | _c1  |
+------+------+
| 3    | 10   |
+------+------+
1 row selected (69.967 seconds)
```

6. Aggregate functions can also be used with the `DISTINCT` keyword to aggregate on unique values:

```
> SELECT
> count(DISTINCT gender_age.gender) as gender_uni_cnt,
> count(DISTINCT name) as name_uni_cnt
> FROM employee;
+-----------------+----------------+
| gender_uni_cnt  | name_uni_cnt   |
+-----------------+----------------+
| 2               | 5              |
+-----------------+----------------+
1 row selected (35.935 seconds)
```

When we use `COUNT` and `DISTINCT` together, it always ignores the setting (such as `mapred.reduce.tasks = 20`) for the number of reducers used and may use only one reducer. In this case, the single reducer becomes the bottleneck when processing large volumes of data. The workaround is to use a subquery as follows:

```
-- May trigger single reducer during the whole processing
> SELECT count(distinct gender_age.gender) as gender_uni_cnt FROM employee;

-- Use subquery to select unique value before aggregations
> SELECT
> count(*) as gender_uni_cnt
> FROM (
> SELECT DISTINCT gender_age.gender FROM employee
) a;
```

In this case, the first stage of the query implementing `DISTINCT` can use more than one reducer. In the second stage, the mapper will have less output just for the `COUNT` purpose, since the data is already unique after implementing `DISTINCT`. As a result, the reducer will not be overloaded.

Sometimes, we may need to find the max. or min. value of particular columns as well as other columns, for example, to answer this question: who are the oldest males and females with ages in the employee table? To achieve this, we can also use max/min on a struct as follows, instead of using subqueries/window functions:

```
> SELECT gender_age.gender,
> max(struct(gender_age.age, name)).col1 as age,
> max(struct(gender_age.age, name)).col2 as name
> FROM employee
> GROUP BY gender_age.gender;
+---------------------+------+------+
| gender_age.gender   | age  | name |
```

```
+--------------------+-----+------+
| Female             | 57  | Lucy |
| Male               | 35  | Will |
+--------------------+-----+------+
2 rows selected (26.896 seconds)
```

Although it still needs to use the GROUP BY clause, this job is more efficient than a regular GROUP BY or subquery, as it only triggers one job.

> The `hive.map.aggr` property controls aggregations in the `map` task. The default value for this setting is `true`, so Hive will do the first-level aggregation directly in the `map` task for better performance, but consume more memory. Turn it off if you run out of memory in the `map` phase.

Enhanced aggregation

Hive offers enhanced aggregation by using the GROUPING SETS, CUBE, and ROLLUP keywords.

Grouping sets

GROUPING SETS implements advanced multiple GROUP BY operations against the same set of data. Actually, GROUPING SETS are a shorthand way of connecting several GROUP BY result sets with UNION ALL. The GROUPING SETS keyword completes all processes in a single stage of the job, which is more efficient. A blank set `()` in the GROUPING SETS clause calculates the overall aggregation. The following are a few examples to show the equivalence of GROUPING SETS. For better understanding, we can say that the outer level (brace) of GROUPING SETS defines what data UNION ALL is to be implemented. The inner level (brace) defines what GROUP BY data is to be implemented in each UNION ALL.

1. Grouping set with one element of column pairs:

```
SELECT
name, start_date, count(sin_number) as sin_cnt
FROM employee_hr
GROUP BY name, start_date
GROUPING SETS((name, start_date));
--||-- equals to
SELECT
name, start_date, count(sin_number) as sin_cnt
FROM employee_hr
```

```
GROUP BY name, start_date;
+---------+------------+---------+
| name    | start_date | sin_cnt |
+---------+------------+---------+
| Lucy    | 2010-01-03 | 1       |
| Michael | 2014-01-29 | 1       |
| Steven  | 2012-11-03 | 1       |
| Will    | 2013-10-02 | 1       |
+---------+------------+---------+
4 rows selected (26.3 seconds)
```

2. Grouping set with two elements:

```
SELECT
name, start_date, count(sin_number) as sin_cnt
FROM employee_hr
GROUP BY name, start_date
GROUPING SETS(name, start_date);
--||-- equals to
SELECT
name, null as start_date, count(sin_number) as sin_cnt
FROM employee_hr
GROUP BY name
UNION ALL
SELECT
null as name, start_date, count(sin_number) as sin_cnt
FROM employee_hr
GROUP BY start_date;
----------+------------+---------+
| name    | start_date | sin_cnt |
+---------+------------+---------+
| NULL    | 2010-01-03 | 1       |
| NULL    | 2012-11-03 | 1       |
| NULL    | 2013-10-02 | 1       |
| NULL    | 2014-01-29 | 1       |
| Lucy    | NULL       | 1       |
| Michael | NULL       | 1       |
| Steven  | NULL       | 1       |
| Will    | NULL       | 1       |
+---------+------------+---------+
8 rows selected (22.658 seconds)
```

3. Grouping set with two elements, a column pair, and a column:

```
SELECT
name, start_date, count(sin_number) as sin_cnt
FROM employee_hr
GROUP BY name, start_date
```

```
GROUPING SETS((name, start_date), name);
--||-- equals to
SELECT
name, start_date, count(sin_number) as sin_cnt
FROM employee_hr
GROUP BY name, start_date
UNION ALL
SELECT
name, null as start_date, count(sin_number) as sin_cnt
FROM employee_hr
GROUP BY name;
+---------+------------+---------+
| name    | start_date | sin_cnt |
+---------+------------+---------+
| Lucy    | NULL       | 1       |
| Lucy    | 2010-01-03 | 1       |
| Michael | NULL       | 1       |
| Michael | 2014-01-29 | 1       |
| Steven  | NULL       | 1       |
| Steven  | 2012-11-03 | 1       |
| Will    | NULL       | 1       |
| Will    | 2013-10-02 | 1       |
+---------+------------+---------+
8 rows selected (22.503 seconds)
```

4. Grouping set with four elements, including all combinations of columns:

```
SELECT
name, start_date, count(sin_number) as sin_cnt
FROM employee_hr
GROUP BY name, start_date
GROUPING SETS((name, start_date), name, start_date, ());
--||-- equals to
SELECT
name, start_date, count(sin_number) as sin_cnt
FROM employee_hr
GROUP BY name, start_date
UNION ALL
SELECT
name, null as start_date, count(sin_number) as sin_cnt
FROM employee_hr
GROUP BY name
UNION ALL
SELECT
null as name, start_date, count(sin_number) as sin_cnt
FROM employee_hr
GROUP BY start_date
UNION ALL
```

```
SELECT
null as name, null as start_date, count(sin_number) as sin_cnt
FROM employee_hr
+-----------+-------------+----------+
| name      | start_date  | sin_cnt  |
+-----------+-------------+----------+
| NULL      | NULL        | 4        |
| NULL      | 2010-01-03  | 1        |
| NULL      | 2012-11-03  | 1        |
| NULL      | 2013-10-02  | 1        |
| NULL      | 2014-01-29  | 1        |
| Lucy      | NULL        | 1        |
| Lucy      | 2010-01-03  | 1        |
| Michael   | NULL        | 1        |
| Michael   | 2014-01-29  | 1        |
| Steven    | NULL        | 1        |
| Steven    | 2012-11-03  | 1        |
| Will      | NULL        | 1        |
| Will      | 2013-10-02  | 1        |
+-----------+-------------+----------+
13 rows selected (24.916 seconds)
```

Rollup and Cube

The ROLLUP statement enables a SELECT statement to calculate multiple levels of aggregations across a specified group of dimensions. The ROLLUP statement is a simple extension of the GROUP BY clause with high efficiency and minimal overhead for a query. Compared to GROUPING SETS, which creates specified levels of aggregations, ROLLUP creates *n+1* levels of aggregations, where *n* is the number of grouping columns. First, it calculates the standard aggregate values specified in the GROUP BY clause. Then, it creates higher-level subtotals, moving from right to left through the list of combinations of grouping columns. For example, GROUP BY a,b,c WITH ROLLUP is equivalent to GROUP BY a,b,c GROUPING SETS ((a,b,c),(a,b),(a),()).

The CUBE statement takes a specified set of grouping columns and creates aggregations for all of their possible combinations. If *n* columns are specified for *CUBE,* there will be 2^n combinations of aggregations returned. For example, GROUP BY a,b,c WITH CUBE is equivalent to GROUP BY a,b,c GROUPING SETS ((a,b,c),(a,b),(b,c),(a,c),(a),(b),(c),()).

The GROUPING__ID function works as an extension to distinguish entire rows from each other. It returns the decimal equivalent of the BIT vector for each column specified after GROUP BY. The returned decimal number is converted from a binary of ones and zeros, which represents whether the column is aggregated (0) in the row or not (1). On the other hand, the grouping(...) function also indicates whether a column in a GROUP BY clause is aggregated or not by returning the binary of 1 or 0 directly. In the following example, the order of columns starts from counting the nearest column (such as name) from GROUP BY. The first row in the result set indicates that none of the columns are being used in GROUP BY.

Compare the following example with the last example in the GROUPING SETS section for a better understanding of GROUPING_ID and grouping(...):

```
SELECT
name, start_date, count(employee_id) as emp_id_cnt,
GROUPING__ID,
grouping(name) as gp_name,
grouping(start_date) as gp_sd
FROM employee_hr
GROUP BY name, start_date
WITH CUBE ORDER BY name, start_date;
```

name	start_date	emp_id_cnt	gid	gp_name	gp_sd
NULL	NULL	4	3	1	1
NULL	2010-01-03	1	2	1	0
NULL	2012-11-03	1	2	1	0
NULL	2013-10-02	1	2	1	0
NULL	2014-01-29	1	2	1	0
Lucy	NULL	1	1	0	1
Lucy	2010-01-03	1	0	0	0
Michael	NULL	1	1	0	1
Michael	2014-01-29	1	0	0	0
Steven	NULL	1	1	0	1
Steven	2012-11-03	1	0	0	0
Will	NULL	1	1	0	1
Will	2013-10-02	1	0	0	0

```
13 rows selected (55.507 seconds)
```

Aggregation condition

Since v0.7.0, HAVING has been added to support the conditional filtering of aggregation results directly. By using HAVING, we can avoid using a subquery after the GROUP BY statement. See the following example:

```
> SELECT
> gender_age.age
> FROM employee
> GROUP BY gender_age.age
> HAVING count(*)=1;
+----------------+
| gender_age.age |
+----------------+
| 27             |
| 30             |
| 35             |
| 57             |
+----------------+
4 rows selected (25.829 seconds)

> SELECT
> gender_age.age,
> count(*) as cnt -- Support use column alias in HAVING, like ORDER BY
> FROM employee
> GROUP BY gender_age.age HAVING cnt=1;
+----------------+-----+
| gender_age.age | cnt |
+----------------+-----+
| 27             | 1   |
| 30             | 1   |
| 35             | 1   |
| 57             | 1   |
+----------------+-----+
4 rows selected (25.804 seconds)
```

 HAVING supports filtering on regular columns too. However, it is recommended to use such a filter type after a WHERE clause rather than HAVING for better performance.

If we do not use `HAVING`, we can use a subquery instead as follows:

```
> SELECT
> a.age
> FROM (
> SELECT count(*) as cnt, gender_age.age
> FROM employee GROUP BY gender_age.age
> ) a WHERE a.cnt <= 1;
+--------+
| a.age  |
+--------+
| 57     |
| 27     |
| 35     |
+--------+
3 rows selected (87.298 seconds)
```

Window functions

Window functions, available since Hive v0.11.0, are a special group of functions that scan multiple input rows to compute each output value. Window functions are usually used with `OVER`, `PARTITION BY`, `ORDER BY`, and the windowing specification. Different from the regular aggregate functions used with the `GROUP BY` clause, and limited to one result value per group, window functions operate on windows where the input rows are ordered and grouped using flexible conditions expressed through an `OVER` and `PARTITION` clause. Window functions give aggregate results, but they do not group the result set. They return the group value multiple times with each record. Window functions offer great flexibility and functionalities compared term the regular `GROUP BY` clause and make special aggregations by HQL easier and more powerful. The syntax for a window function is as follows:

```
Function (arg1,..., argn) OVER ([PARTITION BY <...>] [ORDER BY <....>]
[<window_expression>])
```

`Function (arg1,..., argn)` can be any function in the following four categories:

- **Aggregate Functions**: Regular aggregate functions, such as `sum(...)`, and `max(...)`
- **Sort Functions**: Functions for sorting data, such as `rank(...)`, and `row_number(...)`
- **Analytics Functions**: Functions for statistics and comparisons, such as `lead(...)`, `lag(...)`, and `first_value(...)`

The OVER [PARTITION BY <...>] clause is similar to the GROUP BY clause. It divides the rows into groups containing identical values in one or more partitions by columns. These logical groups are known as partitions, which is not the same term as used for partition tables. Omitting the PARTITION BY statement applies the operation to all the rows in the table.

The [ORDER BY <....>] clause is the same as the regular ORDER BY clause. It makes sure the rows produced by the PARTITION BY clause are ordered by specifications, such as ascending or descending order.

Next, we'll learn more details of each category of window functions through examples.

Window aggregate functions

Using regular aggregate functions in window functions brings more flexibility than GROUP BY, which requires all grouped columns in the select list. Since Hive v2.2.0, DISTINCT has been supported for use with aggregate functions in window functions:

1. Prepare the table and data for demonstration:

```
> CREATE TABLE IF NOT EXISTS employee_contract (
> name string,
> dept_num int,
> employee_id int,
> salary int,
> type string,
> start_date date
> )
> ROW FORMAT DELIMITED
> FIELDS TERMINATED BY '|'
> STORED as TEXTFILE;
No rows affected (0.282 seconds)

> LOAD DATD INPATH '/tmp/hivedemo/data/employee_contract.txt'
> OVERWRITE INTO TABLE employee_contract;
No rows affected (0.48 seconds)
```

2. The regular aggregations are used as window functions:

```
> SELECT
> name,
> dept_num as deptno,
> salary,
> count(*) OVER (PARTITION BY dept_num) as cnt,
```

```
> count(distinct dept_num) OVER (PARTITION BY dept_num) as dcnt,
> sum(salary) OVER(PARTITION BY dept_num ORDER BY dept_num) as
sum1,
> sum(salary) OVER(ORDER BY dept_num) as sum2,
> sum(salary) OVER(ORDER BY dept_num, name) as sum3
> FROM employee_contract
> ORDER BY deptno, name;
```

name	deptno	salary	cnt	dcnt	sum1	sum2	sum3
Lucy	1000	5500	5	1	24900	24900	5500
Michael	1000	5000	5	1	24900	24900	10500
Steven	1000	6400	5	1	24900	24900	16900
Wendy	1000	4000	5	1	24900	24900	20900
Will	1000	4000	5	1	24900	24900	24900
Jess	1001	6000	3	1	17400	42300	30900
Lily	1001	5000	3	1	17400	42300	35900
Mike	1001	6400	3	1	17400	42300	42300
Richard	1002	8000	3	1	20500	62800	50300
Wei	1002	7000	3	1	20500	62800	57300
Yun	1002	5500	3	1	20500	62800	62800

```
11 rows selected (111.856 seconds)
```

Window sort functions

Window sort functions provide the sorting data information, such as row number and rank, within specific groups as part of the data returned. The most commonly used sort functions are as follows:

- row_number: Assigns a unique sequence number starting from 1 to each row, according to the partition and order specification.
- rank: Ranks items in a group, such as finding the top *N* rows for specific conditions.
- dense_rank: Similar to rank, but leaves no gaps in the ranking sequence when there are ties. For example, if we rank a match using dense_rank and have two players tied for second place, we would see that the two players were both in second place and that the next person is ranked third. However, the rank function would rank two people in second place, but the next person would be in fourth place.

- `percent_rank`: Uses rank values rather than row counts in its numerator as *(current rank - 1)/(total number of rows - 1)*. Therefore, it returns the percentage rank of a value relative to a group of values.
- `ntile`: Divides an ordered dataset into a number of buckets and assigns an appropriate bucket number to each row. It can be used to divide rows into equal sets and assign a number to each row.

Here are some examples using window sort functions in HQL:

```
> SELECT
> name,
> dept_num as deptno,
> salary,
> row_number() OVER () as rnum, -- sequence in orginal table
> rank() OVER (PARTITION BY dept_num ORDER BY salary) as rk,
> dense_rank() OVER (PARTITION BY dept_num ORDER BY salary) as drk,
> percent_rank() OVER(PARTITION BY dept_num ORDER BY salary) as prk,
> ntile(4) OVER(PARTITION BY dept_num ORDER BY salary) as ntile
> FROM employee_contract
> ORDER BY deptno, name;
```

name	deptno	salary	rnum	rk	drk	prk	ntile
Lucy	1000	5500	7	4	3	0.75	3
Michael	1000	5000	11	3	2	0.5	2
Steven	1000	6400	8	5	4	1.0	4
Wendy	1000	4000	9	1	1	0.0	1
Will	1000	4000	10	1	1	0.0	1
Jess	1001	6000	5	2	2	0.5	2
Lily	1001	5000	6	1	1	0.0	1
Mike	1001	6400	4	3	3	1.0	3
Richard	1002	8000	1	3	3	1.0	3
Wei	1002	7000	3	2	2	0.5	2
Yun	1002	5500	2	1	1	0.0	1

```
11 rows selected (80.052 seconds)
```

Since Hive v2.1.0, we have been able to use aggregate functions in the OVER clause as follows:

```
> SELECT
> dept_num,
> rank() OVER (PARTITION BY dept_num ORDER BY sum(salary)) as rk
> FROM employee_contract
> GROUP BY dept_num;
+----------+----+
```

```
| dept_num | rk |
+----------+----+
| 1000     | 1  |
| 1001     | 1  |
| 1002     | 1  |
+----------+----+
3 rows selected (54.43 seconds)
```

Window analytics functions

Window analytics functions provide extended data analytics, such as getting lag, lead, last, or first rows in the ordered set. The most commonly used analytics functions are as follows:

- cume_dist: Computes the number of rows whose value is smaller than or equal to, the value of the total number of rows divided by the current row, such as *(number of rows ≤ current row)/(total number of rows)*.
- lead: This function, lead(value_expr[,offset[,default]]), is used to return data from the next row. The number (offset) of rows to lead can optionally be specified, one is by default. The function returns [,default] or NULL when the default is not specified. In addition, the lead for the current row extends beyond the end of the window.
- lag: This function, lag(value_expr[,offset[,default]]), is used to access data from a previous row. The number (offset) of rows to lag can optionally be specified, one is by default. The function returns [,default] or NULL when the default is not specified. In addition, the lag for the current row extends beyond the end of the window.
- first_value: It returns the first result from an ordered set.
- last_value: It returns the last result from an ordered set.

Here are some examples using window analytics functions in HQL:

```
> SELECT
> name,
> dept_num as deptno,
> salary,
> cume_dist() OVER (PARTITION BY dept_num ORDER BY salary) as cume,
> lead(salary, 2) OVER (PARTITION BY dept_num ORDER BY salary) as lead,
> lag(salary, 2, 0) OVER (PARTITION BY dept_num ORDER BY salary) as lag,
> first_value(salary) OVER (PARTITION BY dept_num ORDER BY salary) as fval,
> last_value(salary) OVER (PARTITION BY dept_num ORDER BY salary) as lval,
> last_value(salary) OVER (PARTITION BY dept_num ORDER BY salary RANGE
BETWEEN UNBOUNDED PRECEDING AND UNBOUNDED FOLLOWING) as lval2
```

```
> FROM employee_contract
> ORDER BY deptno, salary;
+---------+------+--------+------+------+-----+------+------+-------+
| name    |deptno| salary | cume | lead | lag | fval |lvalue|lvalue2|
+---------+------+--------+------+------+-----+------+------+-------+
| Will    | 1000 | 4000   | 0.4  | 5500 | 0   | 4000 | 4000 | 6400  |
| Wendy   | 1000 | 4000   | 0.4  | 5000 | 0   | 4000 | 4000 | 6400  |
| Michael | 1000 | 5000   | 0.6  | 6400 | 4000| 4000 | 5000 | 6400  |
| Lucy    | 1000 | 5500   | 0.8  | NULL | 4000| 4000 | 5500 | 6400  |
| Steven  | 1000 | 6400   | 1.0  | NULL | 5000| 4000 | 6400 | 6400  |
| Lily    | 1001 | 5000   | 0.33 | 6400 | 0   | 5000 | 5000 | 6400  |
| Jess    | 1001 | 6000   | 0.67 | NULL | 0   | 5000 | 6000 | 6400  |
| Mike    | 1001 | 6400   | 1.0  | NULL | 5000| 5000 | 6400 | 6400  |
| Yun     | 1002 | 5500   | 0.33 | 8000 | 0   | 5500 | 5500 | 8000  |
| Wei     | 1002 | 7000   | 0.67 | NULL | 0   | 5500 | 7000 | 8000  |
| Richard | 1002 | 8000   | 1.0  | NULL | 5500| 5500 | 8000 | 8000  |
+---------+------+--------+------+------+-----+------+------+-------+
11 rows selected (55.203 seconds)
```

For `last_value`, the result (the `lval` column) is a little bit unexpected. This is because the default window clause (introduced in the next section) used is `RANGE BETWEEN UNBOUNDED PRECEDING AND CURRENT ROW`, which, in the example, means the current row will always be the last value. Changing the windowing clause to `RANGE BETWEEN UNBOUNDED PRECEDING AND UNBOUNDED FOLLOWING` gives us the expected result (see the `lval2` column).

Window expression

`[<window_expression>]` is used to further sub-partition the result and apply the window functions. There are two types of windows: Row Type and Range Type.

According to the JIRA at `https://issues.apache.org/jira/browse/HIVE-4797`, the `rank(...)`, `ntile(...)`, `dense_rank(...)`, `cume_dist(...)`, `percent_rank(...)`, `lead(...)`, `lag(...)`, and `row_number(...)` functions do not support being used with a window expression yet.

For row type windows, the definition is in terms of row numbers before or after the current row. The general syntax of the row window clause is as follows:

```
ROWS BETWEEN <start_expr> AND <end_expr>
```

`<start_expr>` can be any one of the following:

- UNBOUNDED PRECEDING
- CURRENT ROW
- N PRECEDING or FOLLOWING

`<end_expr>` can be any one of the following:

- UNBOUNDED FOLLOWING
- CURRENT ROW
- N PRECEDING or FOLLOWING

The following covers more details about using window expressions and their combinations:

- BETWEEN ... AND: Use it to specify the start point and end point for the window. The first expression (before AND) defines the start point and the second expression (after AND) defines the endpoint. If we omit BETWEEN...AND (such as ROWS N PRECEDING or ROWS UNBOUNDED PRECEDING), Hive considers it as the start point, and the endpoint defaults to the current row (see the win6 and win7 columns in the following examples).
- N PRECEDING or FOLLOWING: This indicates N rows before or after the current row.
- UNBOUNDED PRECEDING: This indicates the window starts at the first row of the partition. This is the start point specification and cannot be used as an endpoint specification.
- UNBOUNDED FOLLOWING: This indicates the window ends at the last row of the partition. This is the endpoint specification and cannot be used as a start point specification.
- UNBOUNDED PRECEDING AND UNBOUNDED FOLLOWING: This indicates the first and last row for every row, meaning all rows in the table (see win14 column in the upcoming examples).
- CURRENT ROW: As a start point, CURRENT ROW specifies that the window begins at the current row or value, depending on whether we have specified ROW or RANGE (RANGE is introduced later in this chapter). In this case, the endpoint cannot be M PRECEDING. As an endpoint, CURRENT ROW specifies that the window ends at the current row or value, depending on whether we have specified ROW or RANGE. In this case, the start point cannot be N FOLLOWING.

The following is a diagram that can help us understand the preceding definitions more clearly:

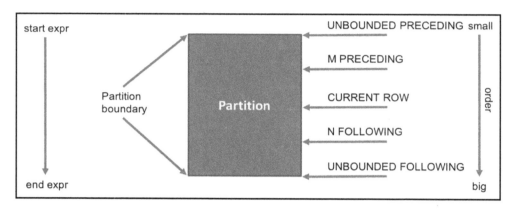

Window expression definitions

The following examples implement the window expressions in row type:

```
-- Preceding and Following
> SELECT
> name, dept_num as dno, salary as sal,
> max(salary) OVER (PARTITION BY dept_num ORDER BY name
> ROWS BETWEEN 2 PRECEDING AND CURRENT ROW) win1,
> max(salary) OVER (PARTITION BY dept_num ORDER BY name
> ROWS BETWEEN 2 PRECEDING AND UNBOUNDED FOLLOWING) win2,
> max(salary) OVER (PARTITION BY dept_num ORDER BY name
> ROWS BETWEEN 1 PRECEDING AND 2 FOLLOWING) win3,
> max(salary) OVER (PARTITION BY dept_num ORDER BY name
> ROWS BETWEEN 2 PRECEDING AND 1 PRECEDING) win4,
> max(salary) OVER (PARTITION BY dept_num ORDER BY name
> ROWS BETWEEN 1 FOLLOWING AND 2 FOLLOWING) win5,
> max(salary) OVER (PARTITION BY dept_num ORDER BY name
> ROWS 2 PRECEDING) win6, -- FOLLOWING does not work in this way
> max(salary) OVER (PARTITION BY dept_num ORDER BY name
> ROWS UNBOUNDED PRECEDING) win7
> FROM employee_contract
> ORDER BY dno, name;
```

name	dno	sal	win1	win2	win3	win4	win5	win6	win7
Lucy	1000	5500	5500	6400	6400	NULL	6400	5500	5500
Michael	1000	5000	5500	6400	6400	5500	6400	5500	5500
Steven	1000	6400	6400	6400	6400	5500	4000	6400	6400
Wendy	1000	4000	6400	6400	6400	6400	4000	6400	6400

Will	1000	4000	6400	6400	4000	6400	NULL	6400	6400
Jess	1001	6000	6000	6400	6400	NULL	6400	6000	6000
Lily	1001	5000	6000	6400	6400	6000	6400	6000	6000
Mike	1001	6400	6400	6400	6400	6000	NULL	6400	6400
Richard	1002	8000	8000	8000	8000	NULL	7000	8000	8000
Wei	1002	7000	8000	8000	8000	8000	5500	8000	8000
Yun	1002	5500	8000	8000	7000	8000	NULL	8000	8000

```
11 rows selected (55.885 seconds)
```

```
-- Current and Unbounded
> SELECT
> name, dept_num as dno, salary as sal,
> max(salary) OVER (PARTITION BY dept_num ORDER BY name
> ROWS BETWEEN CURRENT ROW AND CURRENT ROW) win8,
> max(salary) OVER (PARTITION BY dept_num ORDER BY name
> ROWS BETWEEN CURRENT ROW AND 1 FOLLOWING) win9,
> max(salary) OVER (PARTITION BY dept_num ORDER BY name
> ROWS BETWEEN CURRENT ROW AND UNBOUNDED FOLLOWING) win10,
> max(salary) OVER (PARTITION BY dept_num ORDER BY name
> ROWS BETWEEN UNBOUNDED PRECEDING AND 1 PRECEDING) win11,
> max(salary) OVER (PARTITION BY dept_num ORDER BY name
> ROWS BETWEEN UNBOUNDED PRECEDING AND CURRENT ROW) win12,
> max(salary) OVER (PARTITION BY dept_num ORDER BY name
> ROWS BETWEEN UNBOUNDED PRECEDING AND 1 FOLLOWING) win13,
> max(salary) OVER (PARTITION BY dept_num ORDER BY name
> ROWS BETWEEN UNBOUNDED PRECEDING AND UNBOUNDED FOLLOWING) win14
> FROM employee_contract
> ORDER BY dno, name;
```

name	dno	sal	win8	win9	win10	win11	win12	win13	win14
Lucy	1000	5500	5500	5500	6400	NULL	5500	5500	6400
Michael	1000	5000	5000	6400	6400	5500	5500	6400	6400
Steven	1000	6400	6400	6400	6400	5500	6400	6400	6400
Wendy	1000	4000	4000	4000	4000	6400	6400	6400	6400
Will	1000	4000	4000	4000	4000	6400	6400	6400	6400
Jess	1001	6000	6000	6000	6400	NULL	6000	6000	6400
Lily	1001	5000	5000	6400	6400	6000	6000	6400	6400
Mike	1001	6400	6400	6400	6400	6000	6400	6400	6400
Richard	1002	8000	8000	8000	8000	NULL	8000	8000	8000
Wei	1002	7000	7000	7000	7000	8000	8000	8000	8000
Yun	1002	5500	5500	5500	5500	8000	8000	8000	8000

```
11 rows selected (53.754 seconds)
```

In addition, windows can be defined in a separate window clause or referred to by other windows, as follows:

```
> SELECT
> name, dept_num, salary,
> max(salary) OVER w1 as win1,
> max(salary) OVER w2 as win2,
> max(salary) OVER w3 as win3
> FROM employee_contract
> WINDOW w1 as (
> PARTITION BY dept_num ORDER BY name
> ROWS BETWEEN 2 PRECEDING AND CURRENT ROW
> ),
> w2 as w3,
> w3 as (
> PARTITION BY dept_num ORDER BY name
> ROWS BETWEEN 1 PRECEDING AND 2 FOLLOWING
> );
```

name	dept_num	salary	win1	win2	win3
Lucy	1000	5500	5500	6400	6400
Michael	1000	5000	5500	6400	6400
Steven	1000	6400	6400	6400	6400
Wendy	1000	4000	6400	6400	6400
Will	1000	4000	6400	4000	4000
Jess	1001	6000	6000	6400	6400
Lily	1001	5000	6000	6400	6400
Mike	1001	6400	6400	6400	6400
Richard	1002	8000	8000	8000	8000
Wei	1002	7000	8000	8000	8000
Yun	1002	5500	8000	7000	7000

```
11 rows selected (57.204 seconds)
```

Compared to row type windows, which are in terms of rows, the range type windows are in terms of values in the window expression's specified range. For example, the max(salary) RANGE BETWEEN 500 PRECEDING AND 1000 FOLLOWING statement will calculate max(salary) within the partition by the distance from the current row's value of - 500 to + 1000. If the current row's salary is 4,000, this max(salary) will include rows whose salaries range from 3,500 to 5,000 within each dept_num-specified partition:

```
> SELECT
> dept_num, start_date, name, salary,
> max(salary) OVER (PARTITION BY dept_num ORDER BY salary
> RANGE BETWEEN 500 PRECEDING AND 1000 FOLLOWING) win1,
> max(salary) OVER (PARTITION BY dept_num ORDER BY salary
> RANGE BETWEEN 500 PRECEDING AND CURRENT ROW) win2
> FROM employee_contract
> order by dept_num, start_date;
```

dept_num	start_date	name	salary	win1	win2
1000	2010-01-03	Lucy	5500	6400	5500
1000	2012-11-03	Steven	6400	6400	6400
1000	2013-10-02	Will	4000	5000	4000
1000	2014-01-29	Michael	5000	5500	5000
1000	2014-10-02	Wendy	4000	5000	4000
1001	2013-11-03	Mike	6400	6400	6400
1001	2014-11-29	Lily	5000	6000	5000
1001	2014-12-02	Jess	6000	6400	6000
1002	2010-04-03	Wei	7000	8000	7000
1002	2013-09-01	Richard	8000	8000	8000
1002	2014-01-29	Yun	5500	5500	5500

```
11 rows selected (60.784 seconds)
```

If we omit the *window* expression clause entirely, the default window specification is RANGE BETWEEN UNBOUNDED PRECEDING AND CURRENT ROW. When both ORDER BY and WINDOW expression clauses are missing, the window specification defaults to ROW BETWEEN UNBOUNDED PRECEDING AND UNBOUNDED FOLLOWING.

Sampling

When the data volume is extra large, we may need to find a subset of data to speed up data analysis. This is sampling, a technique used to identify and analyze a subset of data in order to discover patterns and trends in the whole dataset. In HQL, there are three ways of sampling data: random sampling, bucket table sampling, and block sampling.

Random sampling

Random sampling uses the rand() function and LIMIT keyword to get the sampling of data, as shown in the following example. The DISTRIBUTE and SORT keywords are used here to make sure the data is also randomly distributed among mappers and reducers efficiently. The ORDER BY rand() statement can also achieve the same purpose, but the performance is not good:

```
> SELECT name FROM employee_hr
> DISTRIBUTE BY rand() SORT BY rand() LIMIT 2;
+--------+
| name   |
+--------+
| Will   |
| Steven |
+--------+
2 rows selected (52.399 seconds)
```

Bucket table sampling

This is a special sampling method, optimized for bucket tables, as shown in the following example. The SELECT clause specifies the columns to sample data from. The rand() function can also be used when sampling entire rows. If the sample column is also the CLUSTERED BY column, the sample will be more efficient:

```
-- Sampling based on the whole row
> SELECT name FROM employee_trans
> TABLESAMPLE(BUCKET 1 OUT OF 2 ON rand()) a;
+--------+
| name   |
+--------+
| Steven |
+--------+
1 row selected (0.129 seconds)
```

```
-- Sampling based on the bucket column, which is efficient
> SELECT name FROM employee_trans
> TABLESAMPLE(BUCKET 1 OUT OF 2 ON emp_id) a;
+----------+
| name     |
+----------+
| Lucy     |
| Steven   |
| Michael  |
+----------+
3 rows selected (0.136 seconds)
```

Block sampling

This type of sampling allows a query to randomly pick up *n* rows of data, *n* percentage of the data size, or *n* bytes of data. The sampling granularity is the HDFS block size. Refer to the following examples:

```
-- Sample by number of rows
> SELECT name
> FROM employee TABLESAMPLE(1 ROWS) a;
+-----------+
|   name    |
+-----------+
| Michael   |
+-----------+
1 rows selected (0.075 seconds)

-- Sample by percentage of data size
> SELECT name
> FROM employee TABLESAMPLE(50 PERCENT) a;
+-----------+
|   name    |
+-----------+
| Michael   |
| Will      |
+-----------+
2 rows selected (0.041 seconds)

-- Sample by data size
-- Support b/B, k/K, m/M, g/G
> SELECT name FROM employee TABLESAMPLE(1B) a;
+-----------+
|   name    |
+-----------+
| Michael   |
```

```
+----------+
1 rows selected (0.075 seconds)
```

Summary

In this chapter, we covered how to aggregate data using basic aggregation functions. Then, we introduced advanced aggregations with GROUPING SETS, ROLLUP, and CUBE, as well as aggregation conditions using HAVING. We also covered the various window functions. At the end of the chapter, we introduced three ways of sampling data. After going through this chapter, you should be able to do basic and advanced aggregations and data sampling in HQL. In the next chapter, we'll talk about performance considerations in Hive.

Performance Considerations

7

Although Hive is built to deal with big data processing, we still cannot ignore the importance of performance. Most of the time, a better query can rely on the smart query optimizer to find the best execution strategy, as well as the default settings and best practices. However, experienced users should learn more about the theory and practice of performance tuning, especially when working on a performance-sensitive project or environment.

In this chapter, we will start using utilities available in HQL to find potential issues causing poor performance. Then, we introduce the best practices for performance considerations in the areas of design, file format, compression, storage, queries, and jobs. In this chapter, we will cover the following topics:

- Performance utilities
- Design optimization
- Data optimization
- Job optimization

Performance utilities

HQL provides the EXPLAIN and ANALYZE statements, which can be used as utilities to check and identify the performance of queries. In addition, Hive logs contain enough detailed information for performance investigation and troubleshooting.

EXPLAIN statement

Hive provides an EXPLAIN statement to return a query execution plan without running the query. We can use it to analyze queries if we have concerns about their performance. The EXPLAIN statement helps us to see the difference between two or more queries for the same purpose. The syntax for it is as follows:

```
EXPLAIN [FORMATTED|EXTENDED|DEPENDENCY|AUTHORIZATION] hql_query
```

The following keywords can be used:

- FORMATTED: This provides a formatted JSON version of the query plan.
- EXTENDED: This provides additional information for the operators in the plan, such as file pathname.
- DEPENDENCY: This provides a JSON format output that contains a list of tables and partitions that the query depends on. It has been available since Hive v0.10.0
- AUTHORIZATION: This lists all entities needed to be authorized, including input and output to run the query, and authorization failure, if any. It has been available since Hive v0.14.0.

A typical query plan contains the following three sections. We will also have a look at an example later:

- **Abstract Syntax Tree (AST)**: Hive uses a parser generator called ANTLR (see http://www.antlr.org/) to automatically generate a tree syntax for HQL
- **Stage Dependencies**: This lists all dependencies and the number of stages used to run the query
- **Stage Plans**: It contains important information, such as operators and sort orders, for running the job

The following is what a typical query plan looks like. From the following example, we can see that the AST section is shown as a Map/Reduce operator tree. In the STAGE DEPENDENCIES section, both Stage-0 and Stage-1 are independent root stages. In the STAGE PLANS section, Stage-1 has one map and reduce referred to by the Map Operator Tree and Reduce Operator Tree. Inside each Map/Reduce Operator Tree section, all operators corresponding to the query keywords, as well as expressions and aggregations, are listed. The Stage-0 stage does not have map and reduce. It is just a Fetch operation:

```
> EXPLAIN SELECT gender_age.gender, count(*)
> FROM employee_partitioned WHERE year=2018
> GROUP BY gender_age.gender LIMIT 2;
```

```
+----------------------------------------------------------------------+
| Explain                                                              |
+----------------------------------------------------------------------+
| STAGE DEPENDENCIES:                                                  |
| Stage-1 is a root stage                                             |
| Stage-0 depends on stages: Stage-1                                  |
|                                                                      |
| STAGE PLANS:                                                         |
| Stage: Stage-1                                                      |
| Map Reduce                                                          |
| Map Operator Tree:                                                 |
| TableScan                                                          |
| alias: employee_partitioned                                        |
| Pruned Column Paths: gender_age.gender                             |
| Statistics:                                                         |
| Num rows: 4 Data size: 223 Basic stats: COMPLETE Column stats: NONE |
| Select Operator                                                    |
| expressions: gender_age.gender (type: string)                      |
| outputColumnNames: _col0                                           |
| Statistics:                                                         |
| Num rows: 4 Data size: 223 Basic stats: COMPLETE Column stats: NONE |
| Group By Operator                                                 |
| aggregations: count()                                             |
| keys: _col0 (type: string)                                        |
| mode: hash                                                        |
| outputColumnNames: _col0, _col1                                    |
| Statistics:                                                         |
| Num rows: 4 Data size: 223 Basic stats: COMPLETE Column stats: NONE |
| Reduce Output Operator                                            |
| key expressions: _col0 (type: string)                             |
| sort order: +                                                     |
| Map-reduce partition columns: _col0 (type: string)                 |
| Statistics:                                                         |
| Num rows: 4 Data size: 223 Basic stats: COMPLETE Column stats: NONE |
| TopN Hash Memory Usage: 0.1                                        |
| value expressions: _col1 (type: bigint)                            |
| Reduce Operator Tree:                                             |
| Group By Operator                                                 |
| aggregations: count(VALUE._col0)                                  |
| keys: KEY._col0 (type: string)                                    |
| mode: mergepartial                                                |
| outputColumnNames: _col0, _col1                                    |
| Statistics:                                                         |
| Num rows: 2 Data size: 111 Basic stats: COMPLETE Column stats: NONE |
| Limit                                                              |
| Number of rows: 2                                                 |
| Statistics:                                                         |
| Num rows: 2 Data size: 110 Basic stats: COMPLETE Column stats: NONE |
```

```
| File Output Operator                                            |
| compressed: false                                               |
| Statistics:                                                     |
| Num rows: 2 Data size: 110 Basic stats: COMPLETE Column stats: NONE |
| table:                                                          |
| input format:                                                   |
| org.apache.hadoop.mapred.SequenceFileInputFormat                |
| output format:                                                  |
| org.apache.hadoop.hive.ql.io.HiveSequenceFileOutputFormat       |
| serde: org.apache.hadoop.hive.serde2.lazy.LazySimpleSerDe       |
|                                                                 |
| Stage: Stage-0                                                  |
| Fetch Operator                                                  |
| limit: 2                                                        |
| Processor Tree:                                                 |
| ListSink                                                        |
+-----------------------------------------------------------------+
53 rows selected (0.232 seconds)
```

Both the Ambari Hive view and the Hue Hive editor have built-in visualized query explain when running a query. The Ambari Hive view visual the preceding query as follows:

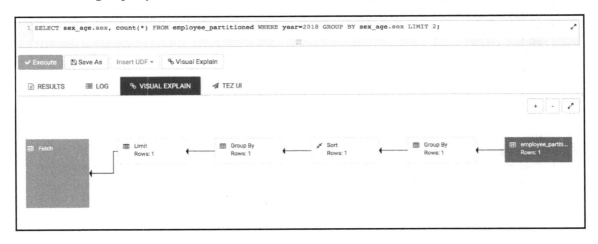

Ambari Hive view visual explaination

ANALYZE statement

Hive statistics are a collection of data that describes more details, such as the number of rows, number of files, and raw data size of the objects in the database. Statistics are the metadata of data, collected and stored in the `metastore` database. Hive supports statistics at the table, partition, and column level. These statistics serve as an input to the Hive **Cost-Based Optimizer** (**CBO**), which is an optimizer used to pick the query plan with the lowest cost in terms of system resources required to complete the query. The statistics are partially gathered automatically in Hive v3.2.0 through to JIRA HIVE-11160 (`https://issues.apache.org/jira/browse/HIVE-11160`) or manually through the `ANALYZE` statement on tables, partitions, and columns, as in the following examples:

1. Collect statistics on the existing table. When the `NOSCAN` option is specified, the command runs faster by ignoring file scanning but only collecting the number of files and their size:

```
> ANALYZE TABLE employee COMPUTE STATISTICS;
No rows affected (27.979 seconds)
> ANALYZE TABLE employee COMPUTE STATISTICS NOSCAN;
No rows affected (25.979 seconds)
```

2. Collect statistics on specific or all existing partitions:

```
-- Applies for specific partition
> ANALYZE TABLE employee_partitioned
> PARTITION(year=2018, month=12) COMPUTE STATISTICS;
No rows affected (45.054 seconds)

-- Applies for all partitions
> ANALYZE TABLE employee_partitioned
> PARTITION(year, month) COMPUTE STATISTICS;
No rows affected (45.054 seconds)
```

3. Collect statistics on columns for existing tables:

```
> ANALYZE TABLE employee_id COMPUTE STATISTICS FOR COLUMNS
employee_id;
No rows affected (41.074 seconds)
```

We can enable automatic gathering of statistics by specifying SET
hive.stats.autogather=true. For new tables or partitions that are
populated through the INSERT OVERWRITE/INTO statement (rather than
the LOAD statement), statistics are automatically collected in the
metastore.

Once the statistics are built and collected, we can check the statistics with the DESCRIBE
EXTENDED/FORMATTED statement. From the table/partition output, we can find the
statistical information inside the parameters, such as parameters:{numFiles=1,
COLUMN_STATS_ACCURATE=true, transient_lastDdlTime=1417726247,
numRows=4, totalSize=227, rawDataSize=223}). The following is an example of
checking statistics in a table:

```
-- Check statistics in a table
> DESCRIBE EXTENDED employee_partitioned PARTITION(year=2018, month=12);

-- Check statistics in a partition
> DESCRIBE EXTENDED employee;
...
parameters:{numFiles=1, COLUMN_STATS_ACCURATE=true,
transient_lastDdlTime=1417726247, numRows=4, totalSize=227,
rawDataSize=223}).

-- Check statistics in a column
> DESCRIBE FORMATTED employee.name;
+--------+---------+---+---+---------+--------------+
|col_name|data_type|min|max|num_nulls|distinct_count| ...
+--------+---------+---+---+---------+--------------+
| name   | string  |   |   | 0       | 5            | ...
+--------+---------+---+---+---------+--------------+
+-----------+-----------+
|avg_col_len|max_col_len| ...
+-----------+-----------+
| 5.6       | 7         | ...
+-----------+-----------+
3 rows selected (0.116 seconds)
```

Logs

Logs provide detailed information to find out how a query/job runs. By checking the log
details, we can identify runtime problems and issues that may cause bad performance.
There are two types of log available, the system log and job log.

The system log contains the Hive running status and issues. It is configured in `{HIVE_HOME}/conf/hive-log4j.properties`. The following three lines of the log properties can be found in the file:

```
hive.root.logger=WARN,DRFA    ## set logger level
hive.log.dir=/tmp/${user.name} ## set log file path
hive.log.file=hive.log        ## set log file name
```

To modify the logger level, we can either modify the preceding property file that applies to all users, or set a Hive command-line config that only applies to the current user session, such as `$hive --hiveconf hive.root.logger=DEBUG,console`.

The job log contains job information and is usually managed by Yarn. To check a job log, use `yarn logs -applicationId <application_id>`.

Design optimization

Design optimization covers several designs, data formats, and job optimization strategies to improve performance. This will be covered in the following sections.

Partition table design

Hive partitioning is one of the most effective ways to improve query performance on larger tables. A query with partition filtering will only load data from the specified partitions (sub-directories), so it can execute much faster than a normal query that filters by a non-partitioning field. The selection of the partition key is always an important factor for performance. It should always be a low-cardinal attribute to avoid so many sub-directories overhead. The following are some attributes commonly used as partition keys:

- **Partitions by date and time**: Use date and time, such as year, month, and day (even hours), as partition keys when data is associated with the date/time columns, such as `load_date`, `business_date`, `run_date`, and so on
- **Partitions by location**: Use country, territory, state, and city as partition keys when data is location related
- **Partitions by business logic**: Use department, sales region, applications, customers, and so on as partition keys when data can be separated evenly by business logic

Bucket table design

Similar to partitioning, a bucket table organizes data into separate files in HDFS. Bucketing can speed up data sampling on buckets. Bucketing can also improve join performance if the join keys are also bucket columns because bucketing ensures the keys are present in a certain bucket. Better-chosen bucket columns make a bucket table join perform better. The best practice for choosing bucket columns is to identify the columns that are most likely used in the filter or join condition in terms of the business logic behind the datasets. For more details, refer to the *Job optimization* section later in this chapter.

Index design

Using indexes is a very common best practice for performance tuning in relational databases. Hive has supported index creation on tables/partitions since Hive v0.7.0. An index in Hive provides a key-based data view and better data access for certain operations, such as WHERE, GROUP BY, and JOIN. Using an index is always a cheaper alternative than full-table scans. The command to create an index in HQL is straightforward, as follows:

```
> CREATE INDEX idx_id_employee_id
> ON TABLE employee_id (employee_id)
> AS 'COMPACT'
> WITH DEFERRED REBUILD;
No rows affected (1.149 seconds)
```

In addition to this COMPACT index, which stores the pair of the indexed column's value and its block ID, HQL has also supported BITMAP indexes since v0.8.0 for column values with less variance, as shown in the following example:

```
> CREATE INDEX idx_gender_employee_id
> ON TABLE employee_id (gender_age)
> AS 'BITMAP'
> WITH DEFERRED REBUILD;
No rows affected (0.251 seconds)
```

The WITH DEFERRED REBUILD option in this example prevents the index from immediately being built. To build the index, we can issue the ALTER...REBUILD commands as shown in the following example. When data in the base table changes, the same command must be used again to bring the index up to date. This is an atomic operation. If the index rebuilt on a table has been previously indexed failed, the state of the index remains the same. See this example to build the index:

```
> ALTER INDEX idx_id_employee_id ON employee_id REBUILD;
```

```
No rows affected (111.413 seconds)

> ALTER INDEX idx_gender_employee_id ON employee_id REBUILD;
No rows affected (82.23 seconds)
```

Once the index is built, a new index table is created for each index with the name in the format of `<database_name>__<table_name>_<index_name>__`:

```
> SHOW TABLES '*idx*';
+------------+----------------------------------------------+-------------+
|TABLE_SCHEM|                 TABLE_NAME                   | TABLE_TYPE|
+------------+----------------------------------------------+-------------+
|default     |default__employee_id_idx_id_employee_id__     |INDEX_TABLE|
|default     |default__employee_id_idx_gender_employee_id__ |INDEX_TABLE|
+------------+----------------------------------------------+-------------+
```

The index table contains the indexed column, the `_bucketname` (a typical file URI on HDFS), and `_offsets` (offsets for each row). Then, this index table can be referred to when we query the indexed columns from the indexed table, as shown here:

```
> DESC default__employee_id_idx_id_employee_id__;
+---------------+-----------------+-----------+
|   col_name    |    data_type    |  comment  |
+---------------+-----------------+-----------+
| employee_id   | int             |           |
| _bucketname   | string          |           |
| _offsets      | array<bigint>   |           |
+---------------+-----------------+-----------+
3 rows selected (0.135 seconds)

> SELECT * FROM default__employee_id_idx_id_employee_id__;
+---------------+-------------------------------------------+-----------+
| employee_id   | _bucketname                               | _offsets  |
+---------------+-------------------------------------------+-----------+
| 100           | .../warehouse/employee_id/employee_id.txt | [0]       |
| 101           | .../warehouse/employee_id/employee_id.txt | [66]      |
| 102           | .../warehouse/employee_id/employee_id.txt | [123]     |
| ...           |                  ...                      | ...       |
+---------------+-------------------------------------------+-----------+
25 rows selected (0.219 seconds)
```

To drop an index, we can only use the `DROP INDEX index_name ON table_name` statement as follows. We cannot drop the index with a `DROP TABLE` statement:

```
> DROP INDEX idx_gender_employee_id ON employee_id;
No rows affected (0.247 seconds)
```

Use skewed/temporary tables

Besides regular internal/external or partition tables, we should also consider using a skewed or temporary table for better design as well as performance.

Since Hive v0.10.0, HQL has supported the creation of a special table for organizing skewed data. A skewed table can be used to improve performance by splitting those skewed values into separate files or directories automatically. As a result, the total number of files or partition folders is reduced. Also, a query can include or ignore this data quickly and efficiently. Here is an example used to create a skewed table:

```
> CREATE TABLE sample_skewed_table (
> dept_no int,
> dept_name string
> )
> SKEWED BY (dept_no) ON (1000, 2000); -- Specify value skewed
No rows affected (3.122 seconds)

> DESC FORMATTED sample_skewed_table;
+------------------+------------------+----------+
| col_name         | data_type        | comment  |
+------------------+------------------+----------+
| ...              | ...              |          |
| Skewed Columns:  | [dept_no]        | NULL     |
| Skewed Values:   | [[1000], [2000]] | NULL     |
| ...              | ...              |          |
+------------------+------------------+----------+
33 rows selected (0.247 seconds)
```

On the other hand, using temporary tables in HQL to keep intermediate data during data recursive processing will save you the effort of rebuilding the common or shared result set. In addition, temporary tables can leverage storage policy settings to use SSD or memory for data storage, and this adds up to better performance too.

Data optimization

Data file optimization covers the performance improvement on the data files in terms of file format, compression, and storage.

File format

Hive supports `TEXTFILE`, `SEQUENCEFILE`, `AVRO`, `RCFILE`, `ORC`, and `PARQUET` file formats. There are two HQL statements used to specify the file format as follows:

- `CREATE TABLE ... STORE AS <file_format>`: Specify the file format when creating a table
- `ALTER TABLE ... [PARTITION partition_spec] SET FILEFORMAT <file_format>`: Modify the file format (definition only) in an existing table

Once a table stored in text format is created, we can load text data directly into it. To load text data into tables that have other file formats, we can first load the data into a table stored as text, where we use `INSERT OVERWRITE/INTO TABLE ... SELECT` to select data from it and then insert the data into the tables that have other file formats.

> To change the default file format for table creation, we can set the `hive.default.fileformat = <file_format>` property for all tables or `hive.default.fileformat.managed = <file_format>` only for internal/managed tables.

`TEXT`, `SEQUENCE`, and `AVRO` files as a row-oriented file storage format are not optimal solutions since the query has to read a full row even if only one column is being requested. On the other hand, a hybrid row-columnar storage file format, such as `RCFILE`, `ORC`, or `PARQUET`, is used to resolve this problem. The details of file formats supported by HQL are as follows:

- `TEXTFILE`: This is the default file format for table creation. Data is stored in clear text for this format. A text file is naturally splittable and able to be processed in parallel. It can also be compressed with algorithms, such as GZip, LZO, and Snappy. However, most compressed files are not splittable for parallel processing. As a result, they use only one job with a single mapper to process data slowly. The best practice for using compressed text files is to make sure the file is not too big and close to a couple of HDFS block sizes.
- `SEQUENCEFILE`: This is a binary storage format for key/value pairs. The benefit of a sequence file is that it is more compact than a text file and fits well with the MapReduce output format. Sequence files can be compressed to record or block level, where the block level has a better compression ratio. To enable block-level compression, we need use do the following settings: `set hive.exec.compress.output=true;` and `set io.seqfile.compression.type=BLOCK;`.

- AVRO: This is also a binary format. More than that, it is also a serialization and deserialization framework. *AVRO* provides a data schema that describes the data structure and also handles the schema changes, such as adding, renaming, and removing columns. The schema is stored along with data for any further processing. Considering AVRO's advantages for dealing with schema evolution, it is recommended to use it when mapping the source data, which is likely to have schema changes time by time.

- RCFILE: This is short for **Record Columnar File**. It is a flat file consisting of binary key/value pairs that share many similarities with a sequence file. The RCFile splits data horizontally into row groups. One or several groups are stored in an HDFS file. Then, RCFile saves the row group data in a columnar format by saving the first column across all rows, then the second column across all rows, and so on. This format is splittable and allows Hive to skip irrelevant parts of the data and get the results faster and cheaper.

- ORC: This is short for Optimized Row Columnar. It has been available since Hive v0.11.0. The ORC format can be considered an improved version of RCFILE. It provides a larger block size of 256 MB by default (RCFILE has 4 MB and SEQUENCEFILE has 1 MB), optimized for large sequential reads on HDFS for more throughput and fewer files to reduce overload in the namenode. Different from RCFILE, which relies on the metastore to know data types, the ORC file understands the data types by using specific encoders so that it can optimize compression depending on different types. It also stores basic statistics, such as MIN, MAX, SUM, and COUNT, on columns as well as a lightweight index that can be used to skip blocks of rows that do not matter.

- PARQUET: This is another row columnar file format that has a similar design to that of ORC. What's more, Parquet has a wider range of support for the majority of projects in the ecosystem, compared to ORC which is mainly supported by Hive, Pig, and Spark. PARQUET leverages the best practices in the design of Google's Dremel (see http://research.google.com/pubs/pub36632.html) to support the nested structure of data. PARQUET has been supported by a plugin since Hive v0.10.0 and got native support after v0.13.0.

Depending on the technology stacks being used, it is suggested to use the ORC format if Hive is the majority tool used to define or process data. If you use several tools in the ecosystem, PARQUET is the better choice in terms of adaptability.

Hadoop Archive File (HAR) is another type of file format to pack HDFS files into archives. This is an option (not a good option) for storing a large number of small-sized files in HDFS, as storing a large number of small-sized files directly in HDFS is not very efficient. However, HAR has other limitations, such as an immutable archive process, not being splittable, and compatibility issues. For more information about HAR and archiving, please refer to the Hive Wiki at https://cwiki.apache.org/confluence/display/Hive/LanguageManual+Archiving.

Compression

Compression techniques in Hive can significantly reduce the amount of data transferring between mappers and reducers by properly compressing intermediate and final output data. As a result, the query will have better performance. To compress intermediate files produced between multiple MapReduce jobs, we need to set the following property (false by default) in the command-line session or the hive-site.xml file:

```
> SET hive.exec.compress.intermediate=true
```

Then, we need to decide which compression codec to configure. A list of commonly supported codecs is in the following table:

Compression	Codec	Extension	Splittable
Deflate	org.apache.hadoop.io.compress.DefaultCodec	.deflate	N
Gzip	org.apache.hadoop.io.compress.GzipCodec	.gz	N
Bzip2	org.apache.hadoop.io.compress.BZip2Codec	.gz	Y
LZO	com.apache.compression.lzo.LzopCodec	.lzo	N
LZ4	org.apache.hadoop.io.compress.Lz4Codec	.lz4	N
Snappy	org.apache.hadoop.io.compress.SnappyCodec	.snappy	N

Deflate (`.deflate`) is a default codec with a balanced compression ratio and CPU cost. The compression ratio for Gzip is very high, as is its CPU cost. Bzip2 is splittable, but it is too slow for compression considering its huge CPU cost, like Gzip. LZO files are not natively splittable, but we can preprocess them (using `com.hadoop.compression.lzo.LzoIndexer`) to create an index that determines the file splits. When it comes to the balance of CPU cost and compression ratio, LZ4 or Snappy do a better job than Deflate, but Snappy is more popular. Since the majority of compressed files are not splittable, it is not suggested to compress a single big file. The best practice is to produce compressed files in a couple of HDFS block sizes so that each file takes less time for processing. The compression codec can be specified in either `mapred-site.xml`, `hive-site.xml`, or a command-line session as follows:

```
> SET hive.intermediate.compression.codec=
org.apache.hadoop.io.compress.SnappyCodec
```

Intermediate compression will only save disk space for specific jobs that require multiple MapReduce jobs. For further saving of disk space, the actual Hive output files can be compressed. When the `hive.exec.compress.output` property is set to `true`, Hive will use the codec configured by the `mapreduce.output.fileoutputformat.compress.codec` property to compress the data in HDFS as follows. These properties can be set in the `hive-site.xml` or in the command-line session:

```
> SET hive.exec.compress.output=true
> SET mapreduce.output.fileoutputformat.compress.codec=
org.apache.hadoop.io.compress.SnappyCodec
```

Storage optimization

Data that is used or scanned frequently can be identified as hot data. Usually, query performance on hot data is critical for overall performance. Increasing the data replication factor in HDFS (see the following example) for hot data could increase the chance of data being hit locally by jobs and improve the overall performance. However, this is a trade-off against storage:

```
$ hdfs dfs -setrep -R -w 4 /user/hive/warehouse/employee
Replication 4 set: /user/hive/warehouse/employee/000000_0
```

On the other hand, too many files or redundancy could make namenode's memory exhausted, especially lots of small files whose sizes are less than the HDFS block sizes. Hadoop itself already has some solutions to deal with many small-file issues in the following ways:

- **Hadoop Archive/**HAR: These are toolkits to pack small files introduced before.
- SEQUENCEFILE **Format**: This is a format that can be used to compress small files into bigger files.
- CombineFileInputFormat: A type of InputFormat to combine small files before map and reduce processing. It is the default InputFormat for Hive (see https://issues.apache.org/jira/browse/HIVE-2245).
- **HDFS Federation**: It supports multiple namenodes to manage more files.

We can also leverage other tools in the Hadoop ecosystem if we have them installed, such as the following:

- HBase has a smaller block size and better file format to deal with smaller file storage and access issues
- Flume NG can be used as a pipe to merge small files into big ones
- Developed and scheduled a file merge program to merge small files in HDFS or before loading the files to HDFS

For Hive, we can use the following configurations to merge files of query results and avoid recreating small files:

- hive.merge.mapfiles: This merges small files at the end of a map-only job. By default, it is true.
- hive.merge.mapredfiles: This merges small files at the end of a MapReduce job. Set it to *true,* as the default is false.
- hive.merge.size.per.task: This defines the size of merged files at the end of the job. The default value is 256,000,000.
- hive.merge.smallfiles.avgsize: This is the threshold for triggering file merge. The default value is 16,000,000.

When the average output file size of a job is less than the value specified by the hive.merge.smallfiles.avgsize property and both hive.merge.mapfiles (for map-only jobs) and hive.merge.mapredfiles (for MapReduce jobs) are set to *true,* Hive will start an additional MapReduce job to merge the output files into big files.

Job optimization

Job optimization covers experience and skills to improve performance in the areas of job-running mode, JVM reuse, job parallel running, and query join optimizations.

Local mode

Hadoop can run in standalone, pseudo-distributed, and fully distributed mode. Most of the time, we need to configure it to run in fully distributed mode. When the data to process is small, it is an overhead to start distributed data processing since the launch time of the fully distributed mode takes more time than the job processing time. Since v0.7.0, Hive has supported automatic conversion of a job to run in local mode with the following settings:

```
> SET hive.exec.mode.local.auto=true; -- default false
> SET hive.exec.mode.local.auto.inputbytes.max=50000000;
> SET hive.exec.mode.local.auto.input.files.max=5; -- default 4
```

A job must satisfy the following conditions to run in local mode:

- The total input size of the job is less than the value set by `hive.exec.mode.local.auto.inputbytes.max`
- The total number of map tasks is less than the value set by `hive.exec.mode.local.auto.input.files.max`
- The total number of reduce tasks required is 1 or 0

JVM reuse

By default, Hadoop launches a new JVM for each map or reduce job and runs the map or reduce task in parallel. When the map or reduce job is a lightweight job running only for a few seconds, the JVM startup process could be a significant overhead. Hadoop has an option to reuse the JVM by sharing the JVM to run mapper/reducer serially instead of in parallel. JVM reuse applies to map or reduce tasks in the same job. Tasks from different jobs will always run in a separate JVM. To enable reuse, we can set the maximum number of tasks for a single job for JVM reuse using the following property. Its default value is 1. If set to -1, there is no limit:

```
> SET mapreduce.job.jvm.numtasks=5;
```

Parallel execution

Hive queries are commonly translated into a number of stages that are executed by the default sequence. These stages are not always dependent on each other. Instead, they can run in parallel to reduce the overall job running time. We can enable this feature with the following settings and set the expected number of jobs running in parallel:

```
> SET hive.exec.parallel=true; -- default false
> SET hive.exec.parallel.thread.number=16; -- default 8
```

Parallel execution will increase cluster utilization. If the utilization of a cluster is already very high, parallel execution will not help much in terms of overall performance.

Join optimization

We have already discussed optimization in different types of Hive joins in Chapter 4, *Data Correlation and Scope*. Here, we'll briefly review the key settings for join improvement.

Common join

The common join is also called the reduce side join. It is a basic join in HQL and works most of the time. For common joins, we need to make sure the big table is on the rightmost side or specified by hit, as follows:

```
/*+ STREAMTABLE(stream_table_name) */
```

Map join

Map join is used when one of the join tables is small enough to fit in the memory, so it is fast but limited by the table size. Since Hive v0.7.0, it has been able to convert map join automatically with the following settings:

```
> SET hive.auto.convert.join=true; -- default true after v0.11.0
> SET hive.mapjoin.smalltable.filesize=600000000; -- default 25m
> SET hive.auto.convert.join.noconditionaltask=true; -- default value above
is true so map join hint is not needed
> SET hive.auto.convert.join.noconditionaltask.size=10000000; -- default
value above controls the size of table to fit in memory
```

Once join auto-convert is enabled, Hive will automatically check whether the smaller table file size is bigger than the value specified by hive.mapjoin.smalltable.filesize, and then it will convert the join to a common join. If the file size is smaller than this threshold, it will try to convert the common join into a map join. Once auto-convert join is enabled, there is no need to provide the map join hints in the query.

Bucket map join

A bucket map join is a special type of map join applied on the bucket tables. To enable a bucket map join, we need to enable the following settings:

```
> SET hive.auto.convert.join=true;
> SET hive.optimize.bucketmapjoin=true; -- default false
```

In a bucket map join, all the join tables must be bucket tables and join on bucket columns. In addition, the bucket number in the bigger tables must be a multiple of the bucket number in the smaller tables.

Sort merge bucket (SMB) join

SMB is a join performed on bucket tables that have the same sorted, bucket, and join condition columns. It reads data from both bucket tables and performs common joins (map and reduce triggered) on the bucket tables. We need to enable the following properties to use SMB:

```
> SET hive.input.format=
> org.apache.hadoop.hive.ql.io.BucketizedHiveInputFormat;
> SET hive.auto.convert.sortmerge.join=true;
> SET hive.optimize.bucketmapjoin=true;
> SET hive.optimize.bucketmapjoin.sortedmerge=true;
> SET hive.auto.convert.sortmerge.join.noconditionaltask=true;
```

Sort merge bucket map (SMBM) join

An SMBM join is a special bucket join but triggers a map-side join only. It can avoid caching all rows in the memory like a map join does. To perform SMBM joins, the join tables must have the same bucket, sort, and join condition columns. To enable such joins, we need to enable the following settings:

```
> SET hive.auto.convert.join=true;
> SET hive.auto.convert.sortmerge.join=true
> SET hive.optimize.bucketmapjoin=true;
> SET hive.optimize.bucketmapjoin.sortedmerge=true;
> SET hive.auto.convert.sortmerge.join.noconditionaltask=true;
> SET hive.auto.convert.sortmerge.join.bigtable.selection.policy=
org.apache.hadoop.hive.ql.optimizer.TableSizeBasedBigTableSelectorForAutoSMJ;
```

Skew join

When working with data that has a highly uneven distribution, data skew could happen in such a way that a small number of compute nodes must handle the bulk of the computation. The following setting informs Hive to optimize properly if data skew happens:

```
> SET hive.optimize.skewjoin=true; --If there is data skew in join, set it
to true. Default is false.
```

```
> SET hive.skewjoin.key=100000;
 --This is the default value. If the number of key is bigger than
 --this, the new keys will send to the other unused reducers.
```

> Skewed data could occur with the GROUP BY data too. To optimize it, we need set hive.groupby.skewindata=true to use the preceding settings to enable skew data optimization in the GROUP BY result. Once configured, Hive will first trigger an additional MapReduce job whose map output will randomly distribute to the reducer to avoid data skew.

For more information about join optimization, please refer to the Hive Wiki at https://cwiki.apache.org/confluence/display/Hive/LanguageManual+JoinOptimization and https://cwiki.apache.org/confluence/display/Hive/Skewed+Join+Optimization.

Job engine

Hive supports running jobs on different engines. The choice of engine will also impact the overall performance. However, this is a bigger change compared to the other settings. Also, this change requires a service restart rather than temporarily make it effective in command-line session. Here is the syntax to set the engine as well as details for each of them:

```
SET hive.execution.engine=<engine>; -- <engine> = mr|tez|spark
```

- mr: This is the default engine, MapReduce. It was deprecated after Hive v2.0.0.
- tez: Tez (http://tez.apache.org/) is an application framework built on Yarn that can execute complex **Directed Acyclic Graphs** (**DAG**s) for general data-processing tasks. Tez further splits map and reduce jobs into smaller tasks and combines them in a flexible and efficient way for execution. Tez is considered a flexible and powerful successor to the MapReduce framework. Tez is production-ready and being used most of the time to replace the mr engine.

- `spark`: Spark is another general purpose big data framework. Its component, Spark SQL, supports a subset of HQL and provides similar syntax to HQL. By using Hive over Spark, Hive can leverage Spark's in-memory computing model as well as Hive's mature cost-based optimizer. However, Hive over Spark requires manual configurations and still lacks solid use cases in production. For more details of Hive over Spark, refer to the Wiki page at (`https://cwiki.apache.org/confluence/display/Hive/Hive+on+Spark%3A+Getting+Started`).

- `mr3`: MR3 is another experiment engine (`https://mr3.postech.ac.kr/`). It is similar to Tez but with the enhancements of simpler design, better performance, and more features. MR3 is documented as ready for production use and supports all major features from Tez, such as Kerberos-based security, authentication and authorization, fault tolerance, and recovery. However, it lacks a solid production use case and best practices in production deployment, as well as CDH or HDP distribution support.

> **Live Long And Process** (**LLAP**) functionality was added in Hive v2.0.0. It combines a live long running query service and intelligent in-memory caching to deliver fast queries. Together with a job engine, LLAP provides a hybrid execution model to improve overall Hive performance. LLAP needs to work through Apache Slider (`https://slider.incubator.apache.org/`) and only works with Tez for now. In the future, it will support other engines. The recent HDP has provided LLAP supported thought Tez.

Optimizer

Similar to relational databases, Hive generates and optimizes each query's logical and physical execution plan before submitting for final execution. There are two major optimizers now in Hive to further optimize query performance in general, Vectorize and **Cost-Based Optimization** (**CBO**).

Vectorization optimization

Vectorization optimization processes a larger batch of data at the same time rather than one row at a time, thus significantly reducing computing overhead. Each batch consists of a column vector that is usually an array of primitive types. Operations are performed on the entire column vector, which improves the instruction pipelines and cache use. Files must be stored in the ORC format in order to use vectorization. For more details on vectorization, please refer to the Hive Wiki (`https://cwiki.apache.org/confluence/display/Hive/Vectorized+Query+Execution`). To enable vectorization, we need to use the following setting:

```
> SET hive.vectorized.execution.enabled=true; -- default false
```

Cost-based optimization

CBO in Hive is powered by Apache Calcite (`http://calcite.apache.org/`), which is an open source, enterprise-grade cost-based logical optimizer and query execution framework. Hive CBO generates efficient execution plans by examining the query cost, which is collected by ANALYZE statements or the metastore itself, ultimately cutting down on query execution time and reducing resource utilization. To use CBO, set the following properties:

```
> SET hive.cbo.enable=true; -- default true after v0.14.0
> SET hive.compute.query.using.stats=true; -- default false
> SET hive.stats.fetch.column.stats=true; -- default false
> SET hive.stats.fetch.partition.stats=true; -- default true
```

Summary

In this chapter, we first covered how to identify performance bottlenecks using EXPLAIN and ANALYZE statements. Then, we spoke about design optimization for performance when using tables, partitions, and indexes. We also covered data file optimization including file format, compression and storage. At the end of this chapter, we discussed job optimization, job engines, and optimizers. After going through this chapter, you should be able to do performance troubleshooting and tuning in Hive. In the next chapter, we'll talk about function extensions for Hive.

Extensibility Considerations

8

Although Hive has provided many built-in functions, in special use cases, users may need power beyond what's provided. In this case, we can extend Hive's functionality in three main areas:

- **User-defined function** (**UDF**): This provides a way to extend functionalities with an external function (mainly written in Java) that can be evaluated in HQL
- **HPL/SQL**: This provides procedure-language-programming support to HQL
- **Streaming**: This plugs a user's own customized programs in to the data streaming
- **SerDe**: This stands for serialization and deserialization and provides a way to serialize or deserialize data with the customized file format

In this chapter, we'll talk about each of them in more detail.

User-defined functions

User-defined functions provide a way to use the user's own application/business logic for processing column values during an HQL query. For example, a user-defined function could perform feature cleaning with an external machine learning library, authenticate user access from other services, merge several values into one or many, perform special data encoding or encryption, and other operations that are outside the scope of the regular HQL operators and functions. Hive defines the following three types of user-defined functions, which are extensible:

- UDF: It stands for User-Defined Function, which operates row-wise and outputs one result for one row, such as most built-in mathematics and string functions.
- UDAF: It stands for User-Defined Aggregating Function, which operates row-wise or group-wise and outputs one row for the whole table or one row for each group as a result, such as the max(...) and count(...) built-in functions.

- UDTF: It stands for User-Defined Table-Generating Function, which also operates row-wise, but produces multiple rows/tables as a result, such as the explode(...) function. UDTF can be used after the SELECT or LATERAL VIEW statement.

 Although all In functions in HQL are implemented in Java, UDF can also be implemented in any JVM-compatible language, such as Scala. In this book, we only focus on writing user-defined functions in Java.

In the following sections, we'll start looking at the Java code template for each kind of user-defined function in more detail.

UDF code template

The code template for a regular UDF is as follows:

```java
package com.packtpub.hive.essentials.hiveudf;

import org.apache.hadoop.hive.ql.exec.UDF;
import org.apache.hadoop.hive.ql.exec.Description;
import org.apache.hadoop.hive.ql.udf.UDFType;
import org.apache.hadoop.io.Text;
// Other libraries my needed

// These information is show by "desc function <function_name>"
@Description(
 name = "udf_name",
 value = "_FUNC_(arg1, ... argN) - description for the function.",
 extended = "decription with more details, such as syntax, examples."
)
@UDFType(deterministic = true, stateful = false)

public class udf_name extends UDF {
    // evaluate() is the only necessary function to overwrite
    public Text evaluate(){
        /*
        * Here to impelement core function logic
        */
        return "return the udf result";
    }
    // override is supported
    public String evaluate(<Type_arg1> arg1,..., <Type_argN> argN){
        /*
```

```
 * Do something here
 */
    return "return the udf result";
  }
}
```

In the preceding template, the package definition and imports should be self-explanatory. We can import whatever is needed besides the top three mandatory libraries. The @Description annotation is a useful Hive-specific annotation to provide function usage. The information defined in the value property will be shown in the DESC FUNCTION statement. The information defined in the extended property will be shown in the DESCRIBE FUNCTION EXTENDED statement. The @UDFType annotation specifies what behavior is expected from the function. A deterministic UDF (deterministic = true) is a function that always gives the same result when passing the same arguments, such as length(...) and max(...). On the other hand, a non-deterministic (deterministic = false) UDF can return a different result for the same set of arguments, for example, unix_timestamp(), which returns the current timestamp in the default time zone. The stateful (stateful = true) property allows functions to keep some static variables available across rows, such as row_number(), which assigns sequential numbers for table rows.

All UDF should extend from the org.apache.hadoop.hive.ql.exec.UDF class, so the UDF subclass has to implement the evaluate() method which can also be overridden for a different purpose. In this method, we can implement expected function logic and exception-handling using Java, Hadoop, and Hive libraries and data types.

UDAF code template

In this section, we introduce the UDAF code template, which extends from the org.apache.hadoop.hive.ql.exec.UDAF class. The code template is as follows:

```
package com.packtpub.hive.essentials.hiveudaf;

import org.apache.hadoop.hive.ql.exec.UDAF;
import org.apache.hadoop.hive.ql.exec.UDAFEvaluator;
import org.apache.hadoop.hive.ql.exec.Description;
import org.apache.hadoop.hive.ql.udf.UDFType;

@Description(
  name = "udaf_name",
  value = "_FUNC_(arg1, arg2, ... argN) - description for the function",
  extended = "description with more details, such as syntax, examples."
```

```
)
@UDFType(deterministic = false, stateful = true)

public final class udaf_name extends UDAF {
  /**
   * The internal state of an aggregation function.
   *
   * Note that this is only needed if the internal state
   * cannot be represented by a primitive type.
   *
   * The internal state can contain fields with types like
   * ArrayList<String> and HashMap<String,Double> if needed.
   */
  public static class UDAFState {
    private <Type_state1> state1;
    private <Type_stateN> stateN;
  }

  /**
   * The actual class for doing the aggregation. Hive will
   * automatically look for all internal classes of the UDAF
   * that implements UDAFEvaluator.
   */
  public static class UDAFExampleAvgEvaluator implements UDAFEvaluator {

    UDAFState state;

    public UDAFExampleAvgEvaluator() {
      super();
      state = new UDAFState();
      init();
    }

    /**
     * Reset the state of the aggregation.
     */
    public void init() {
      /*
       * Examples for initializing state.
       */
      state.state1 = 0;
      state.stateN = 0;
    }

    /**
     * Iterate through one row of original data.
     *
     * The number and type of arguments need to be the same as we
```

```
 * call this UDAF from the Hive command line.
 *
 * This function should always return true.
 */
public boolean iterate(<Type_arg1> arg1,..., <Type_argN> argN){
  /*
   * Add logic here for how to do aggregation if there is
   * a new value to be aggregated.
   */
  return true;
}


/**
 * Called on the mapper side on different data nodes.
 * Terminate a partial aggregation and return the state.
 * If the state is a primitive, just return primitive Java
 * classes like Integer or String.
 */
public UDAFState terminatePartial() {
  /*
   * Check and return a partial result in expectations.
   */
  return state;
}


/**
 * Merge with a partial aggregation.
 *
 * This function should always have a single argument,
 * which has the same type as the return value of
 * terminatePartial().
 */
public boolean merge(UDAFState o) {
  /*
   * Define operations how to merge the result calculated
   * from all data nodes.
   */
  return true;
}


/**
 * Terminates the aggregation and returns the final result.
 */
public long terminate() {
  /*
   * Check and return final result in expectations.
   */
  return state.stateN;
```

```
        }
      }
    }
```

A UDAF must be a subclass of `org.apache.hadoop.hive.ql.exec.UDAF` containing one or more nested static classes implementing `org.apache.hadoop.hive.ql.exec.UDAFEvaluator`. Make sure that the inner class that implements `UDAFEvaluator` is defined as public. Otherwise, Hive won't be able to use reflection and determine the `UDAFEvaluator` implementation. We should also implement the five required functions, `init()`, `iterate()`, `terminatePartial()`, `merge()`, and `terminate()`, which have already been described.

> Both `UDF` and `UDAF` can also be implemented by extending from the `GenericUDF` and `GenericUDAFEvaluator` classes to avoid using Java reflection for better performance. In addition, generic functions support complex data types, such as `MAP`, `ARRAY`, and `STRUCT`, as arguments, while the `UDF` and `UDAF` functions do not. For more information about `GenericUDAF`, please refer to the Hive wiki at `https://cwiki.apache.org/confluence/display/Hive/GenericUDAFCaseStudy`.

UDTF code template

To implement `UDTF`, there is only one method extending from `org.apache.hadoop.hive.ql.exec.GenericUDTF`. There is no plain `UDTF` class. We need to implement three methods: `initialize()`, `process()`, and `close()`. The `UDTF` will call the `initialize()` method, which returns the information of the function output, such as data type and number of output. Then, the `process()` method is called to perform core function logic with arguments and forward the result. Finally, the `close()` method will do a proper cleanup if needed. The code template for `UDTF` is as follows:

```
package com.packtpub.hive.essentials.hiveudtf;

import org.apache.hadoop.hive.ql.udf.generic.GenericUDTF;
import org.apache.hadoop.hive.ql.exec.Description;
import org.apache.hadoop.hive.ql.exec.UDFArgumentException;
import org.apache.hadoop.hive.ql.metadata.HiveException;
import org.apache.hadoop.hive.serde2.objectinspector.ObjectInspector;
import
org.apache.hadoop.hive.serde2.objectinspector.ObjectInspectorFactory;
import
org.apache.hadoop.hive.serde2.objectinspector.PrimitiveObjectInspector;
```

```
import org.apache.hadoop.hive.serde2.objectinspector.StructObjectInspector;
import
org.apache.hadoop.hive.serde2.objectinspector.primitive.PrimitiveObjectInsp
ectorFactory;

@Description(
 name = "udtf_name",
 value = "_FUNC_(arg1, arg2, ... argN) - description for the function",
 extended = "description with more detail, such as syntax, examples."
)
public class udtf_name extends GenericUDTF {
  private PrimitiveObjectInspector stringOI = null;
  /**
   * This method will be called exactly once per instance.
   * It performs any custom initialization logic we need.
   * It is also responsible for verifying the input types and
   * specifying the output types.
   */
  @Override
  public StructObjectInspector initialize(ObjectInspector[] args)
  throws UDFArgumentException {
    // Check number of arguments.
    if (args.length != 1) {
      throw new UDFArgumentException(
      "The UDTF should take exactly one argument");
    }
    /*
     * Check that the input ObjectInspector[] array contains a
     * single PrimitiveObjectInspector of the Primitive type,
     * such as String.
     */
    if (args[0].getCategory() != ObjectInspector.Category.PRIMITIVE
        &&
        ((PrimitiveObjectInspector) args[0]).getPrimitiveCategory()
        !=
        PrimitiveObjectInspector.PrimitiveCategory.STRING) {
        throw new UDFArgumentException(
        "The UDTF should take a string as a parameter");
    }

    stringOI = (PrimitiveObjectInspector) args[0];
    /*
     * Define the expected output for this function, including
     * each alias and types for the aliases.
     */
    List<String> fieldNames = new ArrayList<String>(2);
    List<ObjectInspector> fieldOIs = new ArrayList<ObjectInspector>(2);
    fieldNames.add("alias1");
```

```
        fieldNames.add("alias2");
        fieldOIs.add(PrimitiveObjectInspectorFactory.
                javaStringObjectInspector);
        fieldOIs.add(PrimitiveObjectInspectorFactory.
                javaIntObjectInspector);
        //Set up the output schema.
        return ObjectInspectorFactory.
        getStandardStructObjectInspector(fieldNames, fieldOIs);
    }

    /**
     * This method is called once per input row and generates
     * output. The "forward" method is used (instead of
     * "return") in order to specify the output from the function.
     */
    @Override
    public void process(Object[] record) throws HiveException {
        /*
         * We may need to convert the object to a primitive type
         * before implementing customized logic.
         */
        final String recStr = (String) stringOI.
        getPrimitiveJavaObject(record[0]);

        //Emit newly created structs after applying customized logic.
        forward(new Object[] {recStr, Integer.valueOf(1)});
    }

    /**
     * This method is for any cleanup that is necessary before
     * returning from the UDTF. Since the output stream has
     * already been closed at this point, this method cannot
     * emit more rows.
     */
    @Override
    public void close() throws HiveException {
        //Do nothing.
    }
}
```

Development and deployment

We'll go through the whole development and deployment steps with an example. Let's create a simple function called `toUpper`, which converts a string to uppercase, by following development and deployment steps:

1. Download and install a Java IDE, such as Eclipse or IntelliJ IDEA.
2. Start the IDE and create a Java project
3. Right-click on the project to choose the **Build Path** | **Configure Build Path** | **Add External Jars** option. It will open a new window. Navigate to the directory with the library of Hive and Hadoop. Then, select and add all JAR files we need to import. We can also resolve the library dependency automatically by using Maven (http://maven.apache.org/); the proper pom.xml file is given in the sample code for this book to import as a maven project.
4. In the IDE, create the following ToUpper.java file according to the UDF template mentioned previously:

```
package hive.essentials.hiveudf;
import org.apache.hadoop.hive.ql.exec.UDF;
import org.apache.hadoop.io.Text;
class ToUpper extends UDF {
  public Text evaluate(Text input) {
    if(input == null) return null;
    return new Text(input.toString().toUpperCase());
  }
}
```

5. Compile and build the project JAR file as `hiveudf-1.0.jar`.
6. Upload the JAR file to HDFS with the `hdfs dfs -put hiveudf-1.0.jar /app/hive/function/` command.
7. Create the function as a temporary function that is only valid in the current session. As of Hive v0.13.0, we can also create a permanent function, which is permanently registered to the metastore and can be referenced in all queries and sessions:

```
> CREATE TEMPORARY FUNCTION tmptoUpper
> as 'com.packtpub.hive.essentials.hiveudf.toupper';
> USING JAR 'hdfs:///app/hive/function/hiveudf-1.0.jar';

> CREATE FUNCTION toUpper -- Create permanent function
> as 'hive.essentials.hiveudf.ToUpper'
> USING JAR 'hdfs:///app/hive/function/hiveudf-1.0.jar';
```

8. Verify and check the function:

```
> SHOW FUNCTIONS ToUpper;
> DESCRIBE FUNCTION ToUpper;
> DESCRIBE FUNCTION EXTENDED ToUpper;
+----------------------------------------------------+
| tab_name                                           |
+----------------------------------------------------+
| toUpper(value) - Returns upper case of value.      |
| Synonyms: default.toupper                          |
| Example:                                           |
| > SELECT toUpper('will');                          |
| WILL                                               |
| Function class:hive.essentials.hiveudf.ToUpper     |
| Function type:PERSISTENT                           |
| Resource:hdfs:///app/hive/function/hiveudf-1.0.jar |
+----------------------------------------------------+
```

9. Reload and use the function in HQL:

```
> RELOAD FUNCTION; -- Reload all invisible functions if needed

> SELECT
> name, toUpper(name) as cap_name, tmptoUpper(name) as cname
> FROM employee;
+---------+----------+----------+
| name    | cap_name | c_name   |
+---------+----------+----------+
| Michael | MICHAEL  | MICHAEL  |
| Will    | WILL     | WILL     |
| Shelley | SHELLEY  | SHELLEY  |
| Lucy    | LUCY     | LUCY     |
+---------+----------+----------+
4 rows selected (0.363 seconds)
```

10. Drop the function when needed:

```
> DROP TEMPORARY FUNCTION IF EXISTS tmptoUpper;
> DROP FUNCTION IF EXISTS toUpper;
```

HPL/SQL

Since Hive v2.0.0, the Hadoop Procedure Language SQL (HPL/SQL) (http://www.hplsql.org/) available to provide store procedure programming in Hive. HPL/SQL supports Hive, Spark SQL, and Impala, and is compatible with Oracle, DB2, MySQL, and TSQL standard. One of its benefits is making the migration of existing database-stored procedures to Hive easy and efficient. Using HPL/SQL does not require Java skills to implement what can be done through UDF mentioned. Compared with UDF, HPL/SQL's performance is a little slower and it is still new for production usage.

The following is an example of creating a stored procedure. HPL/SQL supports the creation of both `Function` and `Procedure`:

```
$ cat getEmpCnt.pl
CREATE PROCEDURE getCount()
BEGIN
DECLARE cnt INT = 0;
SELECT COUNT(*) INTO cnt FROM employee;
PRINT 'Users cnt: ' || cnt;
END;

call getCount(); -- Call a procedure
```

In order to run a procedure, we need to set up the database connection in `hplsql-site.xml` by providing the `hiveserver2` connection URL, as follows. After that, HPL/SQL can use the default connection to submit the procedure statement or file:

SQL `hplsql` command, is in the same folder as the `hive` command, with the `-f` option, as follows:

```
$ cat /opt/hive2/conf/hplsql-site.xml

<configuration>
<property>
<name>hplsql.conn.default</name>
<value>hive2conn</value>
</property>
<property>
<name>hplsql.conn.hive2conn</name>
<value>org.apache.hive.jdbc.HiveDriver;jdbc:hive2://localhost:10500</value>
</property>
</configuration>
```

Then, we can call the HPL:

```
$cd /opt/hive2/bin
$ ./hplsql -f getEmpCnt.pl
SLF4J: Class path contains multiple SLF4J bindings.
...
Open connection: jdbc:hive2://localhost:10500 (1.02 sec)
Starting query
Query executed successfully (569 ms)
Users cnt: 4
```

Streaming

Hive can also leverage the streaming feature in Hadoop to transform data in an alternative way. The streaming API opens an I/O pipe to an external process, such as a script. Then, the process reads data from the standard input and writes the results out through the standard output. In HQL, we can use TRANSFORM clauses directly to embed the mapper and the reducer scripts written in commands, shell scripts, Java, or other programming languages. Although streaming brings overhead by using serialization/deserialization between processes, it provides a simple coding mode for non-Java developers. The syntax of the TRANSFORM clause is as follows:

```
FROM (
    FROM src
    SELECT TRANSFORM '(' expression (',' expression)* ')'
    (inRowFormat)?
    USING 'map_user_script'
    (AS colName (',' colName)*)?
    (outRowFormat)? (outRecordReader)?
    (CLUSTER BY?|DISTRIBUTE BY? SORT BY?) src_alias
)
SELECT TRANSFORM '(' expression (',' expression)* ')'
(inRowFormat)?
USING 'reduce_user_script'
(AS colName (',' colName)*)?
(outRowFormat)? (outRecordReader)?
```

By default, the INPUT values for the user script are as follows:

- Columns transformed to STRING values
- Delimited by a tab
- NULL values converted to the N literal string (differentiates NULL values from empty strings)

By default, the OUTPUT values of the user script are as follows:

- Treated as tab-separated STRING columns
- N will be reinterpreted as NULL
- The resulting STRING column will be cast to the data type specified in the table declaration

These defaults can be overridden with ROW FORMAT. An example of streaming using the Python script upper.py is as follows:

```
$cat upper.py
#!/usr/bin/env python
'''
This is a script to upper all cases
'''
import sys

def main():
    try:
        for line in sys.stdin:
          n = line.strip()
          print n.upper()
    except:
        return None
if __name__ == "__main__":main()
```

Test the script by running it in the normal way, as follows:

```
$ echo "Will" | python upper.py
$ WILL
```

Call the script with HQL:

```
> ADD FILE /tmp/upper.py;
> SELECT
> TRANSFORM (name,work_place[0])
> USING 'python upper.py' as (CAP_NAME,CAP_PLACE)
> FROM employee;
```

```
+-----------+------------+
| cap_name  | cap_place  |
+-----------+------------+
| MICHAEL   | MONTREAL   |
| WILL      | MONTREAL   |
| SHELLEY   | NEW YORK   |
| LUCY      | VANCOUVER  |
| STEVEN    | NULL       |
+-----------+------------+
5 rows selected (30.101 seconds)
```

 The TRANSFORM command is not allowed when SQL standard-based authorization is configured as of Hive v0.13.0.

SerDe

SerDe stands for Serialization and Deserialization. It is the technology used to process records and map them to column data types in Hive tables. To explain the scenario of using SerDe, we need to understand how Hive reads and writes data first.

The process to read data is as follows.

1. Data is read from HDFS.
2. Data is processed by the INPUTFORMAT implementation, which defines the input data split and key/value records. In Hive, we can use CREATE TABLE ... STORED AS <FILE_FORMAT> (see Chapter 9, *Performance Considerations*) to specify which INPUTFORMAT it reads from.
3. The Java Deserializer class defined in SerDe is called to format the data into a record that maps to column and data types in a table.

For an example of reading data, we can use JSON SerDe to read the TEXTFILE format data from HDFS and translate each row of the JSON attribute and value to rows in Hive tables with the correct schema.

The process to write data is as follows:

1. Data (such as using an INSERT statement) to be written is translated by the Serializer class defined in SerDe to the format that the OUTPUTFORMAT class can read.

2. Data is processed by the OUTPUTFORMAT implementation, which creates the RecordWriter object. Similar to the INPUTFORMAT implementation, the OUTPUTFORMAT implementation is specified in the same way as a table where it writes the data.
3. The data is written to the table (data saved in the HDFS).

For an example of writing data, we can write a row-column of data to Hive tables using JSON SerDe, which translates data to a JSON text string saved to the HDFS.

A list of commonly used SerDe (org.apache.hadoop.hive.serde2) supported is as follows:

- LazySimpleSerDe: The default built-in SerDe (org.apache.hadoop.hive.serde2.lazy.LazySimpleSerDe) that's used with the TEXTFILE format. It can be implemented as follows:

```
> CREATE TABLE test_serde_lz
> STORED as TEXTFILE as
> SELECT name from employee;
No rows affected (32.665 seconds)
```

- ColumnarSerDe: This is the built-in SerDe used with the RCFILE and ORC format. It can be used as follows:

```
> CREATE TABLE test_serde_rc
> STORED as RCFILE as
> SELECT name from employee;
No rows affected (27.187 seconds)
> CREATE TABLE test_serde_orc
> STORED as ORC as
> SELECT name from employee;
No rows affected (24.087 seconds)
```

- RegexSerDe: This is the built-in Java regular expression used in SerDe to parse text files. It can be used as follows:

```
> CREATE TABLE test_serde_rex(
> name string,
> gender string,
> age string.
> )
> ROW FORMAT SERDE
> 'org.apache.hadoop.hive.contrib.serde2.RegexSerDe'
> WITH SERDEPROPERTIES(
>    'input.regex' = '([^,]*),([^,]*),([^,]*)',
```

```
>     'output.format.string' = '%1$s %2$s %3$s'
> )
> STORED AS TEXTFILE;
No rows affected (0.266 seconds)
```

- `HBaseSerDe`: This is the built-in SerDe to enable Hive to integrate with HBase. We can map a Hive table to an existing HBase table by leveraging this SerDe for querying as well as inserting data. Make sure the HBase daemons are running before running the following query. More details are introduced in `Chapter 10`, *Working with Other Tools*:

```
> CREATE TABLE test_serde_hb(
> id string,
> name string,
> gender string,
> age string
> )
> ROW FORMAT SERDE
> 'org.apache.hadoop.hive.hbase.HBaseSerDe'
> STORED BY
> 'org.apache.hadoop.hive.hbase.HBaseStorageHandler'
> WITH SERDEPROPERTIES (
> "hbase.columns.mapping"=
> ":key,info:name,info:gender,info:age"
> )
> TBLPROPERTIES("hbase.table.name" = "test_serde");
No rows affected (0.387 seconds)
```

- `AvroSerDe`: This is the built-in SerDe that enables reading and writing Avro (see `http://avro.apache.org/`) data in Hive tables. Avro is a remote-procedure-call and data-serialization framework. As of Hive v0.14.0, Avro-backed tables can simply be created by specifying the file format as `AVRO`, in three ways:

```
> CREATE TABLE test_serde_avro( -- Specify schema directly
> name string,
> gender string,
> age string
> )
> STORED as AVRO;
No rows affected (0.31 seconds)

> CREATE TABLE test_serde_avro2 -- Specify schema from properties
> STORED as AVRO
> TBLPROPERTIES (
>    'avro.schema.literal'='{
>      "type":"record",
```

```
>     "name":"user",
>     "fields":[
>     {"name":"name", "type":"string"},
>     {"name":"gender", "type":"string", "aliases":["gender"]},
>     {"name":"age", "type":"string", "default":"null"}
>     ]
>   }'
> );
No rows affected (0.41 seconds)

-- Using schema file directly as follows is a more flexiable way
> CREATE TABLE test_serde_avro3 -- Specify schema from schema
file
> STORED as AVRO
> TBLPROPERTIES (
> 'avro.schema.url'='/tmp/schema/test_avro_schema.avsc'
> );
No rows affected (0.21 seconds)

-- Check the schema file
$ cat /tmp/schema/test_avro_schema.avsc
{
   "type" : "record",
   "name" : "test",
   "fields" : [
     {"name":"name", "type":"string"},
     {"name":"gender", "type":"string", "aliases":["gender"]},
     {"name":"age", "type":"string", "default":"null"}
   ]
}
```

- `ParquetHiveSerDe`: This is the built-in SerDe (`parquet.hive.serde.ParquetHiveSerDe`) that enables reading and writing the Parquet data format as of Hive v0.13.0. It can be used as follows:

```
CREATE TABLE test_serde_parquet
> STORED as PARQUET as
> SELECT name from employee;
No rows affected (34.079 seconds)
```

- `OpenCSVSerDe`: This is the SerDe to read and write CSV data. It comes as a built-in SerDe as of Hive v0.14.0. `OpenCSVSerDe` is more powerful than the built-in row delimiter supported by supporting escape and quote specifications and so on. It can be used as follows:

```
> CREATE TABLE test_serde_csv(
> name string,
```

```
> gender string,
> age string
>)
> ROW FORMAT SERDE
> 'org.apache.hadoop.hive.serde2.OpenCSVSerde'
> WITH SERDEPROPERTIES (
>    "separatorChar" = "\t",
>    "quoteChar" = "'",
>    "escapeChar" = "\\"
> )
> STORED AS TEXTFILE;
```

- `JSONSerDe`: JSON SerDe is available as of Hive v0.12.0 to read and write JSON data records with Hive:

```
> CREATE TABLE test_serde_js(
> name string,
> gender string,
> age string
> )
> ROW FORMAT SERDE
> 'org.apache.hive.hcatalog.data.JsonSerDe'
> STORED AS TEXTFILE;
No rows affected (0.245 seconds)
```

Hive also allows users to define a customized SerDe if none of these work for their data format. For more information about custom SerDe, please refer to the Hive Wiki at `https://cwiki.apache.org/confluence/display/Hive/DeveloperGuide#DeveloperGuide-HowtoWriteYourOwnSerDe`.

Summary

In this chapter, we introduced four main areas to extend Hive's functionalities. We also covered three kinds of user-defined functions as well as their coding templates and deployment steps to guide the coding and deployment process. Then, we introduced HPL/SQL, which adds procedure-language programming to HQL. In addition, we talked about streaming to plug in your own code, which does not have to be Java code. At the end of this chapter, we discussed the available SerDe to parse different formats of data files when reading or writing data. After going through this chapter, you should be able to write basic UDFs and HPL/SQL, plug code into streams, and use available SerDe in Hive.

In the next chapter, we'll talk about security considerations.

Security Considerations **9**

For most open source software, security is a critical area to address before production release. As the leading SQL-like interface for Hadoop data, Hive must ensure that data is securely protected and accessed. For this reason, security in Hive is always considered an integral and important part of the ecosystem. The earlier version of Hive mainly relied on HDFS for security. The security of Hive gradually became mature after `hiveserver2` was released.

This chapter will discuss Hive security in the following areas:

- Authentication
- Authorization
- Mask and encryption

Authentication

Authentication is the process of verifying the identity of a user by obtaining the user's credentials. Hive has offered authentication since `hiveserver2`. In the old version of Hive, `hiveserver1` does not support Kerberos authentication for thrift clients. As result, if we could access the host/port over the network, we could access the server. Instead, we can leverage the `metastore` server, which supports Kerberos, for authentication. In this section, we will briefly talk about authentication configurations in both the `metastore` server and `hiveserver2`.

Kerberos is a network authentication protocol developed by MIT as part of Project Athena. It uses time-sensitive tickets that are generated using symmetric key cryptography to securely authenticate a user in an unsecured network environment. Kerberos, in Greek mythology, was the three-headed dog that guarded the gates of Hades. The three-headed part refers to the three parties involved in the Kerberos authentication process: client, server, and **Key Distribution Center** (**KDC**). All clients and servers registered to KDC are known as a realm, which is typically the domain's DNS name in all caps. For more information, please refer to the MIT Kerberos website: http://web.mit.edu/kerberos/.

Metastore authentication

To force clients to authenticate with the metastore server using Kerberos, we can set the following three properties in the hive-site.xml file and then restart the metastore server to make it work:

1. Enable the **Simple Authentication and Security Layer** (**SASL**) framework to enforce client Kerberos authentication, as follows:

```
<property>
<name>hive.metastore.sasl.enabled</name>
<value>true</value>
<description>If true, the metastore thrift interface will be
secured with SASL framework. Clients must authenticate with
Kerberos.</description>
</property>
```

2. Specify the Kerberos keytab generated. Override the following example if you want to keep the file in other places. Make sure the keytab file permission mask is set to read-only permission (600) to avoid accidentally being changed or deleted. It should also be owned by the same account (hive by default) used to run the metastore server:

```
<property>
<name>hive.metastore.kerberos.keytab.file</name>
<value>/etc/hive/conf/hive.keytab</value>
<description>The sample path to the Kerberos Keytab file
containing the metastore thrift server's service principal.
</description>
</property>
```

3. Specify the Kerberos principal pattern string. The _HOST special string will be replaced automatically with the correct hostname. The YOUR-REALM.COM value should be replaced by the actual realm name:

```
<property>
<name>hive.metastore.kerberos.principal</name>
<value>hive/_HOST@YOUR-REALM.COM</value>
<description>The service principal for metastore server.
</description>
</property>
```

Hiveserver2 authentication

hiveserver2 supports multiple authentication modes, such as Kerberos, LDAP, PAM, and customized code. To configure hiveserver2 to use one of these authentication modes, we can set the proper properties in hive_site.xml as follows, and then restart the hiveserver2 service to make it work:

- NONE: None authentication is what's in the default settings. None here means it allows anonymous access using the following setting:

```
<property>
<name>hive.server2.authentication</name>
<value>NONE</value>
</property>
```

- KERBEROS: If Kerberos authentication is used, it is used to authenticate between the thrift client and hiveserver2 and hiveserver2 and secured the HDFS. To enable Kerberos authentication for hiveserver2, we can set the following properties by specifying the keytab path and the actual realm name in YOUR-REALM.COM:

```
<property>
<name>hive.server2.authentication</name>
<value>KERBEROS</value>
</property>
<property>
<name>hive.server2.authentication.kerberos.keytab</name>
<value>/etc/hive/conf/hive.keytab</value>
</property>
<property>
<name>hive.server2.authentication.kerberos.principal</name>
<value>hive/_HOST@YOUR-REALM.COM</value>
</property>
```

Once Kerberos is enabled, the JDBC client (such as Beeline) must include the principal parameter in the JDBC connection string, such as `jdbc:hive2://hiveserver2host:10000/default;principal=hive/_HOST@REALM`. For more examples of the supported connection string syntax, refer to `https://community.hortonworks.com/articles/4103/hiveserver2-jdbc-connection-url-examples.html`.

- LDAP: To configure `hiveserver2` to use user and password validation backed by LDAP (see `https://en.wikipedia.org/wiki/Lightweight_Directory_Access_Protocol`), we can set the following properties:

```
<property>
<name>hive.server2.authentication</name>
<value>LDAP</value>
</property>
<property>
<name>hive.server2.authentication.ldap.url</name>
<value>LDAP_URL, such as ldap://ldaphost@company.com</value>
</property>
<property>
<name>hive.server2.authentication.ldap.Domain</name>
<value>Domain Name</value>
</property>
```

To configure it with `OpenLDAP` (`https://en.wikipedia.org/wiki/OpenLDAP`), we can add the `baseDN` setting instead of the preceding `Domain` property, as follows:

```
<property>
<name>hive.server2.authentication.ldap.baseDN</name>
<value>LDAP_BaseDN, such as ou=people,dc=packtpub,dc=com</value>
</property>
```

- CUSTOM: This represents the customized authentication provider for `hiveserver2`. To enable it, configure the settings as follows:

```
<property>
<name>hive.server2.authentication</name>
<value>CUSTOM</value>
</property>
<property>
<name>hive.server2.custom.authentication.class</name>
<value>pluggable-auth-class-name</value>
<description>Customized authentication class name, such as
com.packtpub.hive.essentials.hiveudf.customAuthenticator
</description>
</property>
```

Pluggable authentication with a customized class did not work until the bug (see `https://issues.apache.org/jira/browse/HIVE-4778`) was fixed in Hive v0.13.0.

The following is a sample of a customized class that implements the `org.apache.hive.service.auth.PasswdAuthenticationProvider` interface. The overridden `Authenticate(...)` method has the core logic of how to authenticate a username and password. Make sure to copy the compiled JAR file to `$HIVE_HOME/lib/` so that the preceding settings can work:

```
// customAuthenticator.java
package com.packtpub.hive.essentials.hiveudf;

import java.util.Hashtable;
import javax.security.sasl.AuthenticationException;
import org.apache.hive.service.auth.PasswdAuthenticationProvider;

/*
 * The customized class for hiveserver2 authentication
 */

public class customAuthenticator implements PasswdAuthenticationProvider {

    Hashtable<String, String> authHashTable = null;

    public customAuthenticator () {
        authHashTable = new Hashtable<String, String>();
        authHashTable.put("user1", "passwd1");
        authHashTable.put("user2", "passwd2");
    }

    @Override
    public void Authenticate(String user, String password)
            throws AuthenticationException {

      String storedPasswd = authHashTable.get(user);

      if (storedPasswd != null && storedPasswd.equals(password))
          return;

      throw new AuthenticationException(
      "customAuthenticator Exception: Invalid user");
    }
}
```

- PAM: Since Hive v0.13.0, Hive supports **PAM (Pluggable Authentication Modules)** authentication, which provides the benefit of plugging existing authentication mechanisms in to Hive. Configure the following settings to enable PAM authentication. For more information about how to install PAM, please refer to the *Setting Up hiveserver2* article in the Hive wiki at `https://cwiki.` `apache.org/confluence/display/Hive/` `Setting+Up+HiveServer2#SettingUpHiveServer2-` `PluggableAuthenticationModules(PAM).`

```
<property>
<name>hive.server2.authentication</name>
<value>PAM</value>
</property>
<property>
<name>hive.server2.authentication.pam.services</name>
<value>pluggable-auth-class-name</value>
<description> Set this to a list of comma-separated PAM servicesthat
will be used. Note that a file with the same name as the PAMservice
must exist in /etc/pam.d.</description>
</property>
```

Authorization

Authorization is used to verify whether a user has permission to perform a certain action, such as creating, reading, or writing data or metadata. Hive provides three authorization modes: legacy mode, storage-based mode, and SQL standard-based mode.

Legacy mode

This is the default authorization mode in Hive, providing column- and row-level authorization through HQL statements. However, it is not a completely secure authorization mode and has a couple of limitations. It can be mainly used to prevent good users from accidentally doing bad things rather than preventing malicious user operations. In order to enable legacy authorization mode, we need to set the following properties in `hive-site.xml`:

```
<property>
<name>hive.security.authorization.enabled</name>
<value>true</value>
<description>enables or disable the hive client authorization
</description>
```

```
</property>

<property>
<name>hive.security.authorization.createtable.owner.grants</name>
<value>ALL</value>
<description>the privileges automatically granted to the owner whenever a
table gets created. An example like "select, drop" will grant select and
drop privilege to the owner of the table.
</description>
</property>
```

Since this is not a secure authorization mode, we will not discuss it in any more detail here. For more HQL support in legacy authorization mode, please refer to the Hive wiki at `https://cwiki.apache.org/confluence/display/Hive/Hive+Default+Authorization+-+Legacy+Mode`.

Storage-based mode

The storage-based authorization mode (since Hive v0.10.0) relies on the authorization provided by the storage-layer HDFS, which provides both POSIX and ACL permissions (available since Hive v0.14.0; refer to `https://issues.apache.org/jira/browse/HIVE-7583`). Storage-based authorization is enabled in the `metastore` server; it has a single consistent view of metadata across other applications in the ecosystem. This mode checks user permissions against the POSIX permissions on the corresponding file directories in HDFS. In addition to the POSIX permissions model, HDFS also provides access-control lists described in ACLs on HDFS at `http://hadoop.apache.org/docs/r2.4.0/hadoop-project-dist/hadoop-hdfs/HdfsPermissionsGuide.html#ACLs_Access_Control_Lists`.

Considering its implementation, the storage-based authorization mode only offers authorization at the level of databases, tables, and partitions rather than column- and row-level. With dependency on the HDFS permissions, it lacks the flexibility to manage authorization through HQL statements. To enable storage-based authorization mode, we can set the following properties in the `hive-site.xml` file:

```
<property>
<name>hive.security.authorization.enabled</name>
<value>true</value>
<description>enable or disable the hive client authorization
</description>
</property>

</property>
<name>hive.metastore.pre.event.listeners</name>
```

```
<value>org.apache.hadoop.hive.ql.security.authorization.AuthorizationPreEve
ntListener</value>
<description>This turns on metastore-side security.</description>
</property>

<property>
<name>hive.security.authorization.manager</name>
<value>org.apache.hadoop.hive.ql.security.authorization.StorageBasedAuthori
zationProvider</value>
<description>The class name of the Hive client authorization
manager.</description>
</property>

<property>
<name>hive.security.metastore.authorization.manager</name>
<value>org.apache.hadoop.hive.ql.security.HadoopDefaultMetastoreAuthenticat
or
</value>
<description>authenticator manager class name to be used in the metastore
for authentication.</description>
</property>

<property>
<name>hive.security.metastore.authorization.auth.reads</name>
<value>true</value>
<description>If this is true, metastore authorizer authorizes read actions
on database, table</description>
</property>
```

 With effect from Hive v0.14.0, storage-based authorization also authorizes read privileges on databases and tables by default through the `hive.security.metastore.authorization.auth.reads` property. For more information, please refer to https://issues.apache.org/jira/browse/HIVE-8221.

SQL standard-based mode

For fine-grained access control on a column and row level, we can use SQL standard-based mode, available since Hive v0.13.0. It is similar to relational database authorization by using the GRANT and REVOKE statements to control access through the hiveserver2 configuration. However, tools such as Hive or HDFS commands do not access data through hiveserver2, so SQL standard-based mode cannot authorize their access.

Therefore, it is recommended you use storage-based mode together with SQL standard-based mode to authorize users connecting from various tools. To enable SQL standard-based mode authorization, we can set the following properties in the `hive-site.xml` file:

```
<property>
<name>hive.security.authorization.enabled</name>
<value>true</value>
<description>enable or disable the hive client authorization </description>
</property>

<property>
<name>hive.server2.enable.doAs</name>
<value>false</value>
<description>Allows Hive queries to be run by the user who submits the
query rather than the hive user. Need to turn if off for this SQL standard-
base mode</description>
</property>

<property>
<name>hive.users.in.admin.role</name>
<value>dayongd,administrator</value>
<description>Comma-separated list of users assigned to the ADMIN
role.</description>
</property>

<property>
<name>hive.security.authorization.manager</name>
<value>org.apache.hadoop.hive.ql.security.authorization.plugin.sql</value>
</property>

<property>
<name>hive.security.authenticator.manager</name>
<value>org.apache.hadoop.hive.ql.security.authorization.plugin.sqlstd.SQLSt
dConfOnlyAuthorizerFactory</value>
</property>

<property>
<name>hive.security.metastore.authorization.manager</name>
<value>org.apache.hadoop.hive.ql.security.authorization.StorageBasedAuthori
zationProvider,org.apache.hadoop.hive.ql.security.authorization.MetaStoreAu
thzAPIAuthorizerEmbedOnly</value>
<description>It takes a comma separated list, so we can add
MetaStoreAuthzAPIAuthorizerEmbedOnly along with StorageBasedAuthorization
parameter,if we want to enable that as well</description>
</property>
```

In addition, we need to put the following configurations in `hiveserver2-site.xml`, before restarting `hiveserver2`, to make SQL standard-based authorization effective:

```xml
<configuration>

<property>
<name>hive.security.authorization.enabled</name>
<value>true</value>
<description></description>
</property>

<property>
<name>hive.security.authorization.manager</name
<value>org.apache.hadoop.hive.ql.security.authorization.plugin.sqlstd.SQLSt
dHiveAuthorizerFactory</value>
</property>

<property>
<name>hive.security.authenticator.manager</name>
<value>org.apache.hadoop.hive.ql.security.SessionStateUserAuthenticator</va
lue>
</property>

<property>
<name>hive.metastore.uris</name>
<value>thrift://localhost:9085</value>
<description>Use 9083 for hive1 and 9085 for hive2</description>
</property>

</configuration>
```

 Before restarting `hiveserver2` to enable the preceding setting, do not forget to grant admin roles to the users defined in `hive.users.in.admin.role` using `GRANT admin TO USER <user_name>`.

With SQL standard-based mode authorization, we can manage privileges on two levels: role or object.

The syntax to grant or revoke an authorization at the role level is as follows:

- `GRANT <ROLE_NAME> TO <PRINCIPLES> [ WITH ADMIN OPTION]`
- `REVOKE [ADMIN OPTION FOR] <ROLE_NAME> FROM <PRINCIPLES>`

The usage of the parameters is as follows:

- `<ROLE_NAME>`: This is a comma-separated role name
- `<PRINCIPLES>`: This is a user or a role
- `WITH ADMIN OPTION`: This is optional. Once specified, it makes sure that the user gets the privileges to grant the role to other users/roles

On the other hand, the syntax to grant or revoke an authorization at the object level is as follows:

- `GRANT <PRIVILEGE> ON <OBJECT> TO <PRINCIPLES>`
- `REVOKE <PRIVILEGE> ON <OBJECT> FROM <PRINCIPLES>`

Here, the following parameters are used:

- `<PRIVILEGE>`: This can be `INSERT`, `SELECT`, `UPDATE`, `DELETE`, or `ALL`
- `<PRINCIPLES>`: This can be a user or a role
- `<OBJECT>`: This is a table or a view

For more examples of HQL statements to manage SQL standard-based authorization, please refer to the Hive wiki at `https://cwiki.apache.org/confluence/display/Hive/SQL+Standard+Based+Hive+Authorization#SQLStandardBasedHiveAuthorization-Configuration`.

 Apache Sentry is a highly modular system for providing centralized, fine-grained, role-based authorization to both data and metadata stored on an Apache Hadoop cluster. It can be integrated with Hive to deliver advanced authorization controls. For more information about Sentry, please refer to `https://sentry.apache.org/`. Sentry is usually distributed in the Cloudera CDH package. Another similar project is Apache Ranger (`https://ranger.apache.org/`), which is usually distributed in the Hortonworks HDP package.

Mask and encryption

For sensitive and legally protected data, such as **Personal Identity Information** (**PII**) or **Personal Confidential Information** (**PCI**), it is necessary to store data in encrypted or masked format in the filesystem. Since Hive v0.13.0, its data security features have matured in the areas of data hashing, data masking, and data encryption/decryption functions.

The data-hashing function

Before masking data was supported, the built-in hash function has been an alternative since Hive v1.3.0. A hash function reads an input string and produces a fixed-size alphanumeric output string. Since the output is generally uniquely (very little chance of collision) mapping to the input string, the hashed value is quite often used to secure columns, which are the unique identifiers for joining or comparing data. Built-in function, such as md5(...), sha1(...), and sha2(...), can be used for data hashing in HQL:

```
> SELECT
> name,
> md5(name) as md5_name, -- 128 bit
> sha1(name) as sha1_name, -- 160 bit
> sha2(name, 256) as sha2_name -- 256 bit
> FROM employee;
+---------+----------------------------------+
| name    | md5_name                         |
+---------+----------------------------------+
| Michael | 3e06fa3927cbdf4e9d93ba4541acce86 |
| Will    | 2b80f09163f60ce1774b438e605eb1f9 |
| Shelley | e47e592945f28b3c3891ee9d27ec6b61 |
| Lucy    | 80eb0e612760f756547b660c4c71ba7d |
+---------+----------------------------------+

+------------------------------------------+
| sha1_name                                |
+------------------------------------------+
| f8c38b2167c0ab6d7c720e47c2139428d77d8b6a |
| 3e3e5802bd4cad8e29e144b515307d8204a3202a |
| 2d4cab849437156354d24c9564958e6581711d08 |
| c5c8f32bdf9998e0f692231f4f969085c8dc225b |
+------------------------------------------+

+------------------------------------------------------------------+
| sha2_name                                                        |
+------------------------------------------------------------------+
| f089eaef57aba315bc0e1455985c0c8e40c247f073ce1f4c5a1f8ffde8773176 |
| 6cef4ccc1019d6cee6b9cad39d49cabf808ba2e0665d5832b70c44c09c2dfae0 |
| 1e8b342dde7c90cfbc9634c777b6b59388b6a4bd14274adffbfaeed4b329b26e |
| a3fa95a3b95d421c316f1a9b12c88edcc47896705976764d2652425de98f0c4f |
+------------------------------------------------------------------+
4 rows selected (0.344 seconds)
```

The data-masking function

Since Hive v2.1.0, the data-mask function has been available in SQL as built-in UDF. Masking data is quite often requested for user-sensitive data such as credit card numbers, bank account numbers, and passwords. Different from the hash function, the mask function in SQL can specify masking on partial data, which makes it more flexible when you want to keep part of the data unmasked for better understanding. The following are examples of using various mask functions in HQL:

```
> SELECT
 -- big letter to U, small letter to 1, number to #
> mask("Card-0123-4567-8910", "U", "1", "#") as m0,
 -- mask first n (4) values where X|x for big/small letter, n for number
> mask_first_n("Card-0123-4567-8910", 4) as m1,
 -- mask last n (4) values
> mask_last_n("Card-0123-4567-8910", 4) as m2,
 -- mask everthing except first n(4) values
> mask_show_first_n("Card-0123-4567-8910", 4) as m3,
 -- mask everthing except last n(4) values
> mask_show_last_n("Card-0123-4567-8910", 4) as m4,
 -- return a hash value - sha 256 hex
> mask_hash('Card-0123-4567-8910') as m5
> ;
```

m0	m1	m2
U111-####-####-####	Xxxx-0123-4567-8910	Card-0123-4567-nnnn

m3	m4	m5
Card-nnnn-nnnn-nnnn	Xxxx-nnnn-nnnn-8910	f0679e470f380ce5183ba403ec0e7e64

```
1 row selected (0.146 seconds)
```

The data-encryption function

Since Hive v1.3.0, aes_encrypt(input string/binary, key string/binary) and aes_decrypt(input binary, key string/binary) UDF have been provided to support data encryption and decryption using the AES (Advanced Encryption Standard: http://en.wikipedia.org/wiki/Advanced_Encryption_Standard) algorithm, which is a symmetric 128-bit, block-data encryption technique developed by Belgian cryptographers Joan Daemen and Vincent Rijmen.

The following is an example of using these functions:

```
-- 1st para. is value to encryped/decryped
-- 2nd para. is 128 bit (16 Byte) keys
> SELECT
> name,
> aes_encrypt(name,'1234567890123456') as encrypted,
> aes_decrypt(
> aes_encrypt(name,'1234567890123456'),
> '1234567890123456') as decrypted
> FROM employee;
+---------+------------------------+-----------+
| name    | encrypted              | decrypted |
+---------+------------------------+-----------+
| Michael | ��.b��#����-��I         | Micheal   |
| Will    | "�""��r {cgR�%���       | Will      |
| Shelley | ��W@�Dm�[-�?�           | Shelley   |
| Lucy    | ��/i���x���L�q~         | Lucy      |
+---------+------------------------+-----------+
4 rows selected (0.24 seconds)
```

Other methods

As mentioned previously, we can use Apache Ranger or Sentry for column-level access control to enable more granularity of security. In addition, there are patches available to specify columns-level encoding directly on table-creation statements, such as HIVE 6329 (https://issues.apache.org/jira/browse/HIVE-6329) and HIVE 7934 (https://issues.apache.org/jira/browse/HIVE-7934). At the storage level, Hive can also leverage HDFS encryption (https://issues.apache.org/jira/browse/HDFS-6134), which offers transparent encryption and decryption of data on HDFS. It will meet our requirements if we want to encrypt an entire dataset in HDFS.

Summary

In this chapter, we introduced the Hive security areas of authentication, authorization, mask, and encryption. We covered authentications in the `metastore` server and `hiveserver2`. Then, we talked about default, storage-based, and SQL standard-based mode authorization. At the end of this chapter, we discussed various ways of applying data masks and security in Hive. After going through this chapter, you should be able to address security concerns with different authentication, authorization, and data-mask or security methods.

In the next chapter, we'll talk about using Hive with other tools in the big data ecosystem.

Working with Other Tools **10**

As one of the earliest and most popular SQL-over-Hadoop tools, Hive has many use cases when it works with other tools to offer an end-to-end big data solution. In this chapter, we will discuss how Hive works with other tools in the big data ecosystem for the following areas:

- The JDBC/ODBC connector
- The NoSQL database
- The Hue/Ambari Hive view
- HCatalog
- Oozie
- Spark
- Hivemall

The JDBC/ODBC connector

JDBC/ODBC is one of the most common ways for Hive to work with other tools. Hadoop vendors, such as Cloudera and Hortonworks, offer free Hive JDBC/ODBC drivers so that Hive can be connected through these drivers, which can be found at `https://www.cloudera.com/downloads/connectors/hive/jdbc.html` and `https://hortonworks.com/downloads/#addons`.

We can use these JDBC/ODBC connectors to connect Hive from tools such as the following:

- A command-line utility, such as Beeline, mentioned in `Chapter 2`, *Setting Up the Hive Environment*
- An integrated development environment, such as Oracle SQL Developer, also mentioned in `Chapter 2`, *Setting Up the Hive Environment*
- Data extraction, transformation, loading, and integration tools, such as Talend Open Studio (`https://www.talend.com/products/talend-open-studio/`) and Pentaho (`https://www.hitachivantara.com/go/pentaho.html`)
- Business intelligence, reporting, and visualization tools, such as QlikView (`https://www.qlik.com`) and Tableau (`https://www.tableau.com`)
- Data analysis tools, such as Microsoft Excel with Power Query Add-in

Since the setting up connectors is very straightforward, please refer to the websites of the specific tools for more detailed instructions to connect to Hive.

NoSQL

Hive not only provides a connection for data querying but also can map its external table to a NoSQL database, such as `HBase` or MongoDB, with various storage handlers.

To map an existing table in `HBase`, Hive uses the `HBaseStorageHandler` class in the table-creation statement. An example of creating a Hive external table mapping to an existing `HBase` is as follows:

```
> CREATE TABLE hbase_table_sample(
> id int,
> value1 string,
> value2 string,
> map_value map<string, string>
> )
> STORED BY 'org.apache.hadoop.hive.hbase.HBaseStorageHandler'
> WITH SERDEPROPERTIES ("hbase.columns.mapping" =
":key,cf1:val,cf2:val,cf3")
> TBLPROPERTIES ("hbase.table.name" = "table_name_in_hbase");
```

In this special CREATE TABLE statement, the HBaseStorageHandler class is delegating interaction with the HBase table with HiveHBaseTableInputFormat and HiveHBaseTableOutputFormat. The hbase.columns.mapping property is required to map each table column defined in the statement to the HBase table columns in order. For example, the ID, by order, maps to the HBase table's row key as :key. Sometimes, we may need to generate the proper row key columns using Hive UDF if there is no existing column that can be used as a row key for the HBase table. value1 maps to the val column in the cf1 column family in the HBase table. The Hive MAP data type can be used to access an entire column family. Each row can have a different set of columns, where the column names correspond to the map keys, and the column values correspond to the map values, such as the map_value column. The hbase.table.name property, which is optional, specifies the table name known by HBase. If it is not provided, the Hive and HBase table will have the same name, such as hbase_table_sample.

By mapping HBase tables to Hive, Hive users can insert data into the HBase table, join Hive tables with HBase tables, and query data from HBase directly. For more information about configurations and features in progress about Hive-HBase integration, please refer to the Hive wiki: https://cwiki.apache.org/confluence/display/Hive/HBaseIntegration.

Using the same mechanisms, Hive can map its external table to a collection in MongoDB (https://www.mongodb.com), which is a popular document NoSQL database. To set this up, we need to download the MongoDB storage handler JAR from https://github.com/mongodb/mongo-hadoop or https://mvnrepository.com/artifact/org.mongodb.mongo-hadoop/mongo-hadoop-core/2.0.2. Then create the table in HQL, as follows, to map it to the mongo_sample collection in the default database in MongoDB. Make sure MongoDB is started before this operation:

```
> ADD JAR mongo-hadoop-core-2.0.2.jar;
> CREATE TABLE mongodb_table_sample(
> id int,
> value1 string,
> value2 string
> )
> STORED BY 'com.mongodb.hadoop.hive.MongoStorageHandler'
> WITH SERDEPROPERTIES (
>
'mongo.columns.mapping'='{"id":"_id","value1":"value1","value2":"value2"}')
> TBLPROPERTIES (
> 'mongo.uri'='mongodb://localhost:27017/default.mongo_sample'
> );
```

After that, we can insert or query data like we can in the `HBase` mapping tables. Since Hive v2.3.0, a more generic JDBC driver-storage handler has been provided to make Hive tables map to tables in most JDBC compatible databases. For details, see HIVE-1555 (`https://issues.apache.org/jira/browse/HIVE-1555`).

The Hue/Ambari Hive view

Hue (`http://gethue.com/`) is short for Hadoop User Experience. It is a web interface for making the Hadoop ecosystem easier to use. For Hive users, it offers a unified web interface for easily accessing both HDFS and Hive in an interactive environment. Hue is installed in CDH by default, and it can also be installed in other Hadoop distributions. In addition, Hue adds more programming-friendly features to Hive, such as:

- Highlights HQL keywords
- Autocompletes HQL queries
- Offers live progress and logs for Hive and MapReduce jobs
- Submits several queries and checks progress later
- Browses data in Hive tables through a web-user interface
- Navigates through the metadata
- Registers UDF and adds files/archives through a web-user interface
- Saves, exports, and shares query results
- Creates various charts from query results

The following is a screenshot of the Hive editor interface in Hue:

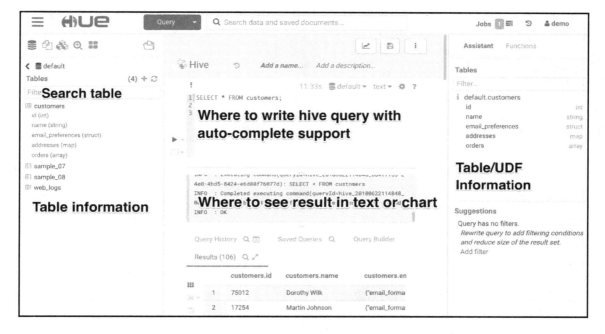

Hue Hive editor user interface

On the other hand, the open source Hadoop cluster-management tool Ambari provides another Hive graphic web-user interface, Hive View (latest version 2). It gives analysts and DBAs a better user experience when performing the following functions in the browser:

- Browse databases and tables
- Write queries or browse query results in full-screen mode
- Manage query execution jobs and history
- View existing databases, tables, and their statistics
- Create tables and export table DDL to source control
- View visual explain plans

The following is a screenshot of the Ambari Hive view version 2:

Ambari Hive view 2

HCatalog

HCatalog (see `https://cwiki.apache.org/confluence/display/Hive/HCatalog`) is a metadata management system for Hadoop data. It stores consistent schema information for Hadoop ecosystem tools, such as Pig, Hive, and MapReduce. By default, HCatalog supports data in the format of `RCFile`, `CSV`, `JSON`, `SequenceFile`, `ORC` file, and a customized format if `InputFormat`, `OutputFormat`, and `SerDe` are implemented. By using HCatalog, users are able to directly create, edit, and expose (via its REST API) metadata, which becomes effective immediately in all tools sharing the same piece of metadata. At first, HCatalog was a separate Apache project from Hive. Eventually, HCatalog became part of the Hive project in 2013 starting with Hive v0.11.0. HCatalog is built on top of the `Hive metastore` and incorporates support for HQL DDL. It provides read and write interfaces and `HCatLoader` and `HCatStorer`. For Pig, it implements Pig's load and store interfaces. HCatalog also provides an interface for MapReduce programs by using `HCatInputFormat` and `HCatOutputFormat`, which are very similar to other customized formats, by implementing Hadoop's `InputFormat` and `OutputFormat`.

In addition, HCatalog provides a REST API from a component called WebHCat so that HTTP requests can be made from other applications to access the metadata of Hadoop MapReduce/Yarn, Pig, and Hive through HCatalog. There is no Hive-specific REST interface since HCatalog uses Hive's `metastore`. Therefore, HCatalog can define metadata for Hive directly through its CLI. The HCatalog CLI supports HQL `SHOW`/`DESCRIBE` statement and the majority of Hive DDL, except the following statements, which require triggering MapReduce jobs:

- `CREATE TABLE ... AS SELECT`
- `ALTER INDEX ... REBUILD`
- `ALTER TABLE ... CONCATENATE`
- `ALTER TABLE ARCHIVE/UNARCHIVE PARTITION`
- `ANALYZE TABLE ... COMPUTE STATISTICS`
- `IMPORT/EXPORT`

Oozie

Oozie (`http://oozie.apache.org/`) is an open source workflow coordination and schedule service to manage data-processing jobs. Oozie workflow jobs are defined in a series of nodes in a **Directed Acyclical Graph** (**DAG**). Acyclical here means that there are no loops in the graph and all nodes in the graph flow in one direction without going back. Oozie workflows contain either the control-flow node or the action node:

- **Control-flow node**: This either defines the start, end, and failed node in a workflow, or controls the workflow execution path, such as decision, fork, and join nodes
- **Action node**: This defines the core data-processing action job, such as MapReduce, Hadoop filesystem, Hive, Pig, Spark, Java, Shell, Email, and Oozie sub-workflows. Additional types of actions are also supported by customized extensions

Oozie is a scalable, reliable, and extensible system. It can be parameterized for workflow submission and scheduled to run automatically. Therefore, Oozie is very suitable for lightweight data integration or maintenance jobs. The core Oozie job requires a workflow-definition XML file and a property file. The following is an example of a workflow XML file using `hive2` action to submit a query. The workflow XML file should be uploaded to HDFS in order to submit a job:

```
<!-- This is Oozie workflow definition -->
<workflow-app xmlns="uri:oozie:workflow:0.5" name="hive2-wf">
    <start to="hive2-node"/>

    <action name="hive2-node">
        <hive2 xmlns="uri:oozie:hive2-action:0.1">
            <job-tracker>${jobTracker}</job-tracker>
            <name-node>${nameNode}</name-node>
            <configuration>
                <property>
                    <name>mapred.job.queue.name</name>
                    <value>${queueName}</value>
                </property>
            </configuration>
            <!-- the hiveserver2 jdbc uri from property file -->
            <jdbc-url>${jdbcURL}</jdbc-url>
            <!-- the hdfs path for the hql -->
            <script>/tmp/hql_script.hql</script>
            <!-- pass parameters to the hql -->
            <param>database=${database}</param>
        </hive2>
        <ok to="end"/>
        <error to="fail"/>
    </action>

    <kill name="fail">
        <message>Failed for [${wf:errorMessage(wf:lastErrorNode())}]
        </message>
    </kill>
    <end name="end"/>
</workflow-app>
```

The following are the job property files for the workflow. The property file should be kept locally:

```
$ cat job.properties
nameNode=hdfs://localhost:8020
jobTracker=localhost:8032
queueName=default
examplesRoot=examples
jdbcURL=jdbc:hive2://localhost:10000/default
database=default
oozie.use.system.libpath=true
oozie.wf.application.path=${nameNode}/user/${user.name}/${examplesRoot}/app
s/hive2
```

We can upload the `workflow.xml` file to the HDFS location defined in the `oozie.wf.application.path` property. Then, run the following command to submit the job and get a job ID for job management or monitoring:

```
$ export OOZIE_URL=http://localhost:11000/oozie
$ oozie job -run -config job.properties
job: 0000001-161213015814745-oozie-oozi-W
```

Spark

As a general-purpose data engine, Apache Spark can integrate with Hive closely. Spark SQL has supported a subset of HQL and can leverage the `Hive metastore` to write or query data in Hive. This approach is also called Spark over Hive. To configure Spark, use Hive the `metastore`, you only need to copy the `hive-site.xml` to the `${SPARK_HOME}/conf` directory. After that, running the `spark-sql` command will enter the Spark SQL interactive environment, where you can write SQL to query Hive tables.

On the other hand, Hive over Spark is a similar approach, but lets Hive use Spark as an alternative engine. In this case, users still stay in Hive and write HQL, but run over the Spark engine transparently. Hive over Spark requires the Yarn `FairScheduler` and `set hive.execution.engine=spark`. For more details, refer to `https://cwiki.apache.org/confluence/display/Hive/Hive+on+Spark%3A+Getting+Started`.

Hivemall

Apache Hivemall (`https://hivemall.incubator.apache.org/`) is a collection of Hive UDFs for machine learning. It contains a number of ML algorithm implementations across classification, regression, recommendations, loss functions, and feature engineering, all as UDFs. This allows end users to use SQL and only SQL to apply machine learning algorithms to a large volume of training data. Perform the following steps to set it up:

1. Download Hivemall from `https://hivemall.incubator.apache.org/download.html` and put it into HDFS:

```
$ hdfs fs -mkdir -p /apps/hivemall
$ hdfs fs -put hivemall-all-xxx.jar /apps/hivemall
```

2. Create permanent functions using script here (`https://github.com/apache/incubator-hivemall/blob/master/resources/ddl/define-all-as-permanent.hive`):

```
> CREATE DATABASE IF NOT EXISTS hivemall; -- create a db for the
udfs
> USE hivemall;
> SET hivevar:hivemall_jar=
> hdfs:///apps/hivemall/hivemall-all-xxx.jar;
> SOURCE define-all-as-permanent.hive;
```

3. Verify the functions are created:

```
> SHOW functions "hivemall.*";
hivemall.adadelta
hivemall.adagrad
...
```

Summary

In this final chapter, we started with the Hive JDBC and ODBC connector. Then, we introduced other popular big data tools and libraries that are often used with Hive, such as NoSQL (HBase, MongoDB), web user interface (Hue, Ambari Hive View), HCatalog, Oozie, Spark, and Hivemall. After going through this chapter, you should now understand how to use other big data tools with Hive to provide end-to-end data intelligence solutions.

Other Books You May Enjoy

If you enjoyed this book, you may be interested in these other books by Packt:

Big Data Analytics with Hadoop 3
Sridhar Alla

ISBN: 978-1-78862-884-6

- Explore the new features of Hadoop 3 along with HDFS, YARN, and MapReduce
- Get well-versed with the analytical capabilities of Hadoop ecosystem using practical examples
- Integrate Hadoop with R and Python for more efficient big data processing
- Learn to use Hadoop with Apache Spark and Apache Flink for real-time data analytics
- Set up a Hadoop cluster on AWS cloud
- Perform big data analytics on AWS using Elastic Map Reduce

Building Data Streaming Applications with Apache Kafka
Manish Kumar, Chanchal Singh

ISBN: 978-1-78728-398-5

- Learn the basics of Apache Kafka from scratch
- Use the basic building blocks of a streaming application
- Design effective streaming applications with Kafka using Spark, Storm &, and Heron
- Understand the importance of a low -latency , high- throughput, and fault-tolerant messaging system
- Make effective capacity planning while deploying your Kafka Application
- Understand and implement the best security practices

Leave a review - let other readers know what you think

Please share your thoughts on this book with others by leaving a review on the site that you bought it from. If you purchased the book from Amazon, please leave us an honest review on this book's Amazon page. This is vital so that other potential readers can see and use your unbiased opinion to make purchasing decisions, we can understand what our customers think about our products, and our authors can see your feedback on the title that they have worked with Packt to create. It will only take a few minutes of your time, but is valuable to other potential customers, our authors, and Packt. Thank you!

Index

CPSIA information can be obtained
at www.ICGtesting.com
Printed in the USA
FSHW010200130819
60979FS

A full list of titles published by Photographers' Institute Press is available by visiting our website, www.pipress.com

All titles are avail   specialist retailers.

                                                                        ct:

PIP, Castl   ed Kingdom

                                                                        ɔm